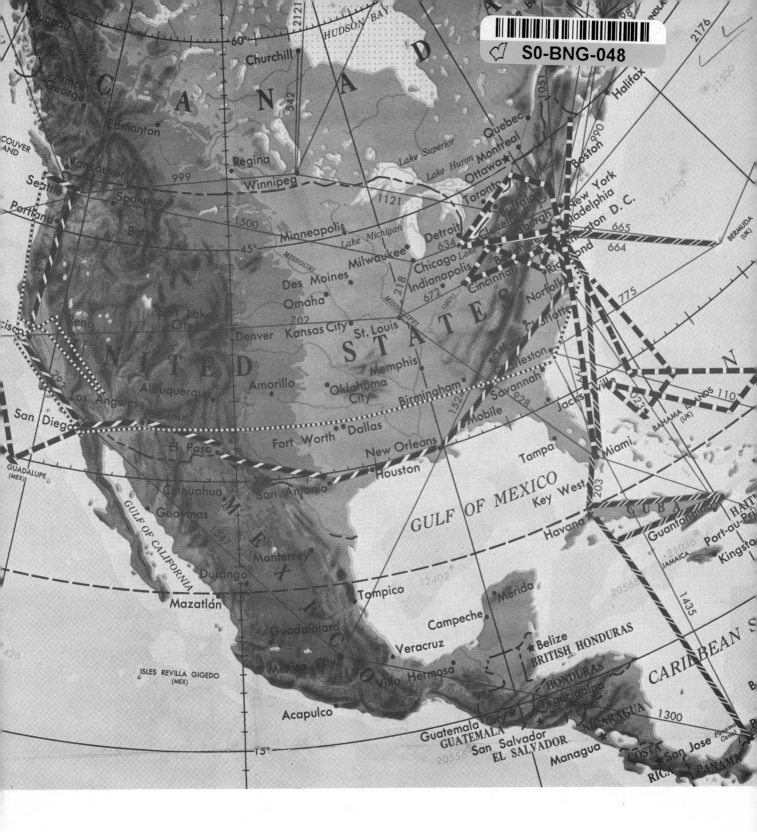

Flight Routes Of The U.S.S. Akron

Commander Frank Carey McCord U.S.N.

Sky Ship

THE AKRON ERA

FAMOUS AIRSHIPS SERIES:

Sky Ship
The AKRON Era

By Thom Hook

AIRSHOW PUBLISHERS
6118 Allwood Court, Baltimore, Maryland 21210

Dedicated to:

Commander Roland G. Mayer, Construction Corps, U.S.N. (Ret.)

By the same author:

"Illustrated FLYING BASICS"
(Eleven editions since 1965)

"Shenandoah Saga"—1973
(Third printing August 1981)

Author Thom Hook (left) and newscaster Paul Harvey (center) with Noble County, Ohio citizens at the Bicentennial Commission's dedication of markers commemmorating *U.S.S. Shenandoah*.
Caldwell Journal photo.

Preface

When I was a boy of nine—the same age as my son, Evan—I was attending a small boarding school on Maryland's Eastern Shore. My playmates at Gunston School, near Centreville, were the two stepsons of Lt. D. Ward Harrigan, senior Heavier-Than-Air (HTA) pilot with the hook-on planes of the *U.S.S. Akron*. This was the airship era, and we were privileged to see that airship and the *Los Angeles* at different times during our period at Gunston. The majestic passage of these slow-moving large silver shapes in the air ocean left an unforgetable impression on all who saw them. There is nothing quite like it today. Perhaps viewing a *C-5A* Galaxy landing or taking off evokes a similar visual impact on the beholder today. But you would have to put three such large aircraft nose-to-tail to equal the size of a large rigid airship, and you still would not have the 15 stories of height to flesh-out the picture of immense size.

Why a book solely on the *Akron,* when accounts of it appear in chapters or parts of existing books? My answer is that it is more appealing to me to follow the story of one vessel than to have a shotgun approach to all airships to make up an account for history. As in the case of my book, "*Shenandoah Saga,*" I felt the reader could develop an affection for a particular airship by knowing the men who flew her, the achievements of the ship as well as the calamaties that came from time to time before the eventual loss of the ship.

Like other children living on the east coast, I was taken to Lakehurst and marvelled at the *Los Angeles* and the blimps housed in the enormous Hangar No. 1, which is now a National Historic Landmark. The *LA* and the *Akron* were each seen from our school on the Corsica river, the former flying low over the grounds on her way eastward and, at a different time, the *Akron* somewhat more distant yet magnificent with the sun shining on her silver-colored hull. After I grew up, I long held the thought that a book describing the training of the "brown shoe men" of Lakehurst would make good reading. The thought lingered over several decades, feeling that someone connected with the LTA program would write such a book. Then, when I came across the various airship files in the National Air and Space Museum, I decided to tackle the job, first with the unravelling of the *Shenandoah* story.

That book was published in late 1973. Then I learned that letters and memorabilia from the widow of Lt. (jg) Hammond James Dugan had been deposited with the Maryland Historical Society. Researching the "Dugan Letters" there, I discovered that Dugan described his training at Lakehurst, his command of the metalclad blimp, *ZMC-2*, his postgraduate schooling dealing with a thesis on the *Akron*, and his eventual flights on that airship. He wrote exceptionally well, and some of his accounts were the basis for articles by his classmate, Hanson Baldwin, the famous military writer for the *New York Times*.

My research has taught me that there really was nothing "light" about LTA other than the hydrogen or helium used to provide lift for airships, blimps and balloons. The men involved had a special appreciation and enthusiasm for a promising type of flight that airplanes did not provide. Even Col. Charles A. Lindbergh and Gen. Billy Mitchell were proponents of airships and went on record before the Congress to see that development continued, citing the relatively few airships available in comparison with airplanes, whose losses did not deter continuation of aircraft development.

This small band of naval officers and men were up against not only the difficulties of flying their big behemoths and more particularly, handling them on the ground in docking and undocking, but had to struggle for acceptance from officers of the Fleet and of Heavier-Than-Air. Theirs was an uphill battle, and they had too few airships to avoid the penalty of disaster.

A memorial to the *Akron* dead was dedicated in the Cathedral of the Air at Lakehurst, N.J. on April 8, 1973–the nearest Sunday to the 40th anniversary of the airship's loss Tuesday morning, April 4, 1933. A Brooklyn firm which had made the memorial tablets for the *U.S.S. Shenandoah's* 14 men killed included an ingot of duralumin from that airship along with commercial grade duralumin in making the *Akron* memorial.

Following the career of Lt. "Red" Dugan, I sense the enjoyment and infatuation these men possessed for the field they had chosen. His experience grows to a crescendo with his assignment to the *Akron*, and the tale is a "people" story rather than strictly a story of "hardware."

"Sky Ship–the *Akron* Era" aims to give tribute to Lt. Dugan and those who gave their lives while staking their careers to a mode of transportation that still offers promise, complementing airplanes, ships and rail for movement of passengers and cargo.

Thom Hook

Table of Contents

Aida D'Acosta, first woman to pilot an airship, is seen guiding Santos-Dumont's Number 9 in flight over Paris six months before the Wright Brothers flew a powered aircraft at Kitty Hawk, North Carolina. *National Air & Space Museum photo.*

CHAPTER ONE

A Time for Eagles

On February 6, 1903, a prominent Maryland Catholic Irish family intent on filling its home with sons and daughters welcomed a third child. This new infant, a male with red hair and gray-green eyes, was a forerunner of more to come. Eventually there would be seven sons and five daughters in the family of Ferdinand Chatard Dugan, a prominent Baltimore lawyer. The baby's mother, Melanie Carroll Boone Dugan, named him Hammond James Dugan, after a relative and early Maryland settler. Family lines went back to Charles Carroll of Carrollton.

The wisteria-festooned victorian home in the Baltimore suburb of Catonsville, on Nunnery Lane, was an exemplary center of the old-fashioned family, filled with love for all. Relatives and friends came and went continuously. The father provided well, and as is often the case with very large families, the Dugan children faced a growing-up experience destined to bring them to adulthood in a well-adjusted status.

That year of 1903 was replete with achievement of a pioneering nature to man's conquest of the air that is worthy of review in order to understand events that occurred decades later.

It was the year the Wright Brothers made their first successful powered flight at Kitty Hawk, North Carolina. Six months before that history-making flight known to every school boy, a charming little man in Paris was creating headlines and gathering admirers, having already built nine airships. He was Alberto Santos-Dumont, a wealthy Brazilian whose nonchalant flights over the City of Lights made his name a household word. A visionary without engineering credentials, he nevertheless pioneered in airship development, starting with a three-horsepower motorcycle engine for

power. Somehow he managed never to have the highly flammable hydrogen that filled his sausage-shaped envelope catch a spark from the engine's exhaust. He had cut his large white teeth on the basics of lighter-than-air flight as a free-balloonist. Of this period of self-training, he describes in his book, *Dans l'Air*, the sensation of being carried into a thunderstorm, which at first scared him considerably. Then he became accustomed to it: "On, on I went, tearing through the blackness. I knew I must be going with great speed, yet sensed no motion. I heard and felt the storm. I realized I was in great danger, yet the danger was not tangible. With it there was a fierce kind of joy. What shall I say? How shall I describe it? Up there in the black solitude, amid the lightning flashes and the thunder claps, I was part of the storm."

By June of 1903, one might meet the dapper little man (he weighed 110 pounds) anywhere in the city in his high collar, derby, kid gloves and peg-topped trousers a couple of inches above his ankles. He flew low over the rooftops and the parks, following his belief that "the place of an airship is not in high altitudes." Then, after each successful flight, he would relax, quite often meeting friends at Maxim's on the Rue Royale. There, in his eager, shrill voice he would engage in lively discussions about all the interesting goings-on of the city. The Eiffel Tower was new—gray instead of rust-colored—and he had used it for a pylon several years earlier in flying from St. Cloud seven miles across Paris. The prize money he gave to the poor of Paris.

A most eligible bachelor of 30, he had no wish to marry, because he wanted to be able to hazard his life in his mission to conquer the air. In his twenties, he had mastered ballooning. His first air-

Testing airship number 5, Santos-Dumont
circles Longchamps racecourse ten times
in July of 1901 for a total of 20 miles,
at 19 miles per hour. Later, Number 5
comes to an end by crashing into the light
well of the Trocadero Hotel, with Santos
hanging 40 feet above ground until rescued.
Below right: Santos-Dumont (seated) and his
artisans in their work shop.
National Air & Space Museum photo

ship had showed his principles were correct. He had but a handful of artisans working for him, and he often rolled up his sleeves to work with them. As time went on, he kept improving his ships, parts of the old one becoming part of a new one each time he needed to modify a component. He built his keel of wood and substituted wire for ropes to get less drag. His developments were not without their anxious moments—gas bags draped over rooftops; being hauled to safety from a dizzying height up a city building; rudder connections breaking for a forced landing, etc. When he crashed airship number 5 into a tree, a Brazilian noblewoman sent the trapped Santos a picnic lunch to see him through the rescue operation.

In June of 1903 a young beauty of Cuban lineage who was well-known in New York society came to Paris. Mademoiselle Aida D'Acosta soon received an introduction to Santos, and expressed a wish to fly. For three different days, he overcame his disinterest in the opposite sex and taught her how to handle the controls and work the engine. On the final lesson, he had airship number 9 on a tether fifty feet above ground, with the engine running.

On June 29, 1903, he sent Aida D'Acosta flying solo as an anxious team of helpers stood by. Santos had helped her with the pilot's preflight check list, of which he was the Father: "Is the balloon properly filled? Any leaks? Condition of the rigging? Motor running smoothly? Do the cords working rudder, motor ballast and the weightshifting guiderope work freely? Is weight okay?" Nothing left to memory, a printed list being the safest way to make certain the airship is ready.

"Let go all!" Mlle. D'Acosta yelled down. Santos borrowed a bicycle and started following her, as number 9 flew slowly from Neuilly to Bagatelle, a half-mile away. He narrowly missed bumping into strollers on the way, his face looking upwards all the way.

The crowd at Bagatelle expected to see Santos running the ship.

"C'est une fille!" the crowd observed.

Mlle. D'Acosta dropped the mooring-rope and made a good landing. Santos congratulated her, and the lovely Aida became the heroine of the city for having made the aeronaut invest time in a member of the opposite sex. She gave him her picture, which he kept in a prominent place on his office desk. But in a few weeks she went back to New York, the first woman to solo in powered flight—*a half year before the Wright Brothers did so.*

Santos-Dumont was in love with flight, and that was his first and last investment of a romantic nature to the ladies. He was too busy designing, changing and flying.

(Years later, Mlle. D'Acosta became Mrs. Henry Breckenridge of Kentucky. Her husband, the colonel, was Charles A. Lindbergh's attorney, and presided at the U.S. Congressional Investigation into the loss of the *Akron*.)

The little Brazilian, with an inheritance from his father, was able to work wholeheartedly at airship design. While little "Red" Dugan was still a baby in Baltimore, Santos-Dumont published his book, *Dans l'Air* in 1904. He visited America for the St. Louis World's Fair but was unable to exhibit his current airship. It had been slashed mysteriously in its crate, ripped beyond repair with a knife. He also met President Theodore Roosevelt, along with U.S. Navy Admirals Dewey, Mahan and Chester. The Admirals, much interested in *le petit Santos'* airships, took him on a tour of the Naval Academy at Annapolis, Maryland. The Navy had heard of the inventive Santos' appearance in his airship the year before over the Army of the Republic in a Grand Review. The were familiar with his prediction that someday there would be great aerostats, as large as ocean-going liners, plying between continents. The military men had also heard of the potential for any steerable lighter-than-air vessel which could scout the enemy's fleet from a safe distance. The well-read French writer, M. Rochefort, wrote: "Suppose the daring Brazilian offered his services to the Boers . . . (he could) observe and transmit details of English troop movement . . . could drop explosive charges in the midst of their lines, and it would be impossible to fight against the devastation."

The days were passing quickly for Santos, who as an aerial sportsman was performing marvelously simple flights in which he would bring his small airship down at a terrace cafe on the Ave. du Bois de Boulogne, coil his guide rope around the legs of his chair and drink an iced orangeade, the big yellow bag just above his knees.

He predicted the time would come when owners of handy little airships would not be having to land in the streets, but would have their ropes caught by

Santos-Dumont's newest airship, number 9, is test flown in experiments with the new egg-shaped form of balloon prior to building a larger airship. It is the smallest airship ever built (11 meters long), with a gas capacity of 340 cubic yards and a Clement air cooled 3½ h.p. engine.
National Air & Space Museum photo.

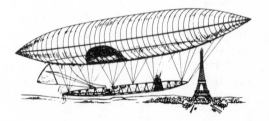

domestics on their own roof gardens. Emergencies, such as engine fires, Santos discovered, could be extinguished if the pilot wore a panama hat with which to beat out the flames.

The year that he visited the Naval Academy he let the Admirals know of the comparison between travel in the air and on the sea. In *Dans l'Air,* he put it this way: "What one feels at sea is not so much the movement . . . as the smell of the paint, varnish, tar, mingled with the odors of the galley, the heat of the boilers, and the stench of the smoke and the hold.

"In the airship, there is no smell—all is pure and clean—and the pitching itself has none of the shocks and hesitations of the boat at sea. Indeed, I can't describe the delight, the wonder, and the intoxication of this free diagonal movement onward and upward or onward and downward."

Meanwhile, Santos was not oblivious to the promise of more powerful yet smaller engines which were now making heavier-than-air (HTA) flight promising. In 1904, with a new mathematics adviser he began design and construction of a box-kite-like flyer. The engine would be between the wings, and the plane would be a canard—with the elevators ahead of the main plane. His airship flying had already convinced him of the need for an artificial horizon in order for the pilot to be able to find his position in the air at any time.

For balance and center of gravity trials, No. 14 *bis* (14a) was pulled along a tightrope by a donkey. It was first taken aloft below the number 14 airship, becoming the world's first "hook-on" airplane, from which the ability to detach or attach in flight would be developed decades later.

In 1905, the pioneer flyer recorded: "I have never made it any secret that to my mind, the first practical use of the airship will be found in war."

October 23, 1906, Santos stood in his new flyer, facing the elevators ahead and by today's standards seemingly with his back to the craft's two big wings. While on previous occasions the undercarriage had collapsed on landing, this time he landed successfully. To Frenchmen, having long disputed the Wright Brothers flight of nearly three years previous, this was the world's first flight.

That flight at Bagatelle was the first for many Europeans. From that moment, Santos-Dumont's work was directed toward Heavier-Than-Air flight. He knew the speed potential of airplanes over airships, and despite his earlier successes, recorded

that propelling "a dirigible balloon through the air is like pushing a candle through a brick wall." He now had no more time nor money to develop the colorful yellow envelopes with their silk covering.

The month following, on November 12, Santos-Dumont won the French Aero Club prize for the first public airplane flight in Europe. His box-kite type craft had an 80 horsepower Antoinette engine and the course was again at Bagatelle, near Paris.

Although it took great courage to fly in a succession of craft of one's own design and manufacture, the pioneer felt that motoring on land was a greater source of getting hurt or killed than flying. Certainly, the odds for colliding were greater on land.

By 1907, Santos-Dumont was no longer the only European pilot of heavier-than-air craft. More than a handful of aviators had joined the ranks of airplane pilots. Some of them had been helped by the Brazilian's ideas, since he shared his information and never patented his discoveries.

While Santos had switched to airplane development, the U.S. Army in August of 1908 purchased its first dirigible airship, for $6,700. A year later, that service purchased its first airplane. The suppliers were the Wright Brothers, and the price $30,000.

The same year, *le petit Santos* flew Number 20, which he named the *Demoiselle*—young girl, or butterfly in translation. His philosophy of design, which was "keep it simple," was evident in the plane's lack of complexity. It was powered by a 35 horsepower engine, and its successful trials were held at St. Cyr, between Paris and Versailles.

On July 25, 1909, Santos' contemporary, the virile Louis Bleriot, crossed the English Channel from Barraques, near Calais, to Dover in a monoplane with a 25 h.p. engine that gave him a speed of 45 miles an hour.

By the middle of 1910, from ten to fifteen copies of the *Demoiselle* were flying, encouraged by Dumont to make use of his design. That same year he had a nervous breakdown from his intense work, which eight years later was found to be not merely from hard work but an incurable disease that fell his lot, known as disseminated sclerosis. Although active in the world of flight and lauded internationally, he never flew again. He was 36 years old and had pioneered in first lighter- and then heavier-than-air flight.

The year that Santos-Dumont stopped flying,

Capt. Wild, circa 1905, climbing above Chicago rooftops in his "Eagle".
National Air and Space Museum photo.

the U.S. Navy established its first aviation camp at Greenbury Point, on the north banks of the Severn River opposite the Academy grounds. There a young officer named John H. Towers, naval aviator number 3, gave instruction in the bamboo pusher planes of the day. On June 20, 1913 the first fatality occurred when a pilot flying with Towers fell out into the Chesapeake Bay. He was Ensign William Billingsley and since at that time seat belts did not exist, Naval Aviator No. 9 was tossed out when the frail seaplane hit turbulence. From that point on the Navy required seatbelts for all pilots.

Across the Severn River from the embryo flight training camp in 1911, two midshipmen were in the regiment undergoing the grueling courses necessary to graduate and become naval officers. Charles Emery Rosendahl, a native of Chicago whose family had moved to Texas, was a plebe; Frank Carey McCord from Vincennes, Indiana, was a first classman, set to graduate. McCord had entered as a plebe at the tender age of 16; he was only 20 when he graduated.

McCord, a strikingly handsome youth with clean-cut features—alert, wide-open eyes—was two years older than Rosendahl and three years ahead of him at the Naval Academy. As was the case of the old "Lucky Bag" yearbooks, the "writers" were greatly concerned with their classmates' proclivity or lack of same for dating. Of McCord, the scribe wrote: ". . . his continued refusal to be enticed to the hops led us to believe in his attachment to some fair one at home."

McCord had finished high school in three years, and the "Lucky Bag" noted that he was "one of the favored ones who can get through on very little boning. Reads novels in study hours and is an inveterate smoker, being particularly fond of bull scags." The write-up also pointed out that McCord was "Of the sort who hoe their own row, doing much and saying little."

Nicknames of "Alice" and "Mac" were pegged to McCord, the former from a popular play of the day called "Alice of Old Vincennes." Despite his handsome, manly features, he would have to carry the cross of "Alice" for years ahead whenever he met his classmates.

Rosendahl's nicknames were "Rosie," "Rabbi" and "Manager." He earned baseball numerals and played championship handball doubles for two years. Of the quotations describing "Rosie," one was from Robert Louis Stevenson: "Such a creature, so fiery, so pugnacious." The other, from Shakespeare, was "Young Cassius hath a lean and hungry look."

While McCord and Rosendahl were matriculating at the Academy—the boyish McCord, younger than most all of his fellow seniors—developments in aviation were taking place abroad. The English military looked into the potential of aviation in the Spring of 1911. A naval flying school was started at Eastchurch, based on a course in flying begun by four British officers. In April 1911, the Air Battalion of the Royal Engineers was formed. It was subdivided into an airship company and an airplane company. The former laid the groundwork for British leadership in non-rigid airship "know-how" prior to World War I and which enabled the English to utilize blimps for patrol successfully over the North Sea.

In Germany, Count Ferdinand von Zeppelin established the first commercial airline in 1911. His *Delag* company operated five ships as time went on, flying 12,000,000 passenger miles without a single injury to passengers.

In 1912, America was not as fortunate as Germany with airships. Five men were killed in an airship called the *Akron* when it exploded at Atlantic City. The highly-flammable hydrogen would continue to bring disasters when used as the lifting gas for airships, including the burning of the first Goodyear blimp, the Wingfoot Express, over Chicago's Loop district, killing 10 airmen.

One of the pioneering aeronauts in England was Edward Maitland-Maitland, who loved parachuting and ballooning. In 1908, accompanied by two other men, he had flown the *Daily Graphic* Balloon from England to Russia. He was the first man to parachute from 10,000 feet, to study the phenomenon of swinging. In 1913, he took Edward, Prince of Wales, on his first flight.

England's war with Germany brought on January 19-20, 1915, the first airship raid on Britain. A pair of Zeppelins dropped bombs at Norfolk. That spring, May 31, 1915, the first Zeppelin raid over London was made. During the war 56 tons of bombs were dropped on London and 214 tons on other parts of the country. On June 7, 1915, a Zeppelin was destroyed in the air over Ghent by Flight Sub-Lieutenant R. A. J. Warneford. He was awarded the Victoria Cross, and died a few days later in an air accident. Another Zeppelin was destroyed in its shed at Evere. All in

U.S. Navy crew of the ill-fated airship *ZR-2 (R-38)*, seen the day before her last flight in England
after 56½ flying hours. Top row, (from left): C.W. Cass, ACMM; A.L. Loftin, ACMM*; W.A. Russell, ACMM***;
F. F. Moorman, ACMM; J. C. Burnett, CY; C. W. Frank, AR1c; C. H. Broom, ACMM**; J. T. Robertson, CRM;
A. E. Carlson, ACR***; R. M. Coons, ACMM*. Second row (from left): J. T. Hancock, ACMM*; M. H. Lay, ACR*;
L. E. Crowl, ACMM*; Norman O. Walker, AR1c (only American survivor); C. S. Solar, AMM1c; Waterman, RM1c;
C. A. Heckbert, AR1c; Ralph Jones, AMM1c; Lester Coleman, ACMM. Bottom row (from left): C. J. Aller, ACR*;
Wm. Lamkey, ACMM; A. B. Galatian, ACMM; Jimmy Shield, ACR; Geo. Welch, ACMM*; J. W. Cullinan, ACMM**;
P. Julius, ACMM*; Christense, ACR; A. D. Pettit, ACR*; S. F. Stevens, ACMM; W. M. Dickinson, ACMM;
W. J. Steele, ACMM*; J. H. Collier, ACR. *Killed on the *ZR-2*: **Killed on the *U.S.S. Shenandoah*;
***Killed on the *U.S.S. Akron*.
Keith Burnett Photo.

The U.S. Naval Academy "Lucky Bag" yearbook for the class of
1924, carries this photo of Hammond James Dugan from Baltimore.
Copy photo from the Maryland Historical Society.

all, five Zeppelins were brought down over Britain in 1916.

During World War I, American naval officers flew blimps with the British over the North Sea. Duty on ships was still the accepted Navy course in a career, and young Frank Carey McCord was a Lieutenant Commander by 1919, commanding a new destroyer, the *U.S.S. McCook.* For his capable handling of his ship and personnel on a cruise from Nantucket to Dalmatia, his superior noted McCord's marked efficiency and the impression made that he was "an excellent officer."

In 1920, while McCord was demonstrating his leadership and skill in commanding ships, Midshipman Ferdinand C. Dugan, second classman at the Naval Academy in Annapolis, welcomed his younger brother, Hammond James Dugan as a plebe.

Young Hammond James Dugan had been appointed June 19, 1920, somehow from the 7th Congressional District of Oklahoma, although he had prepped at Baltimore schools. He played lacrosse and started a big scrapbook containing mementoes of life at the Academy. "Red" or "Jim" was a regular American boy, and as his plebe year was about to end, he received a letter from the Superintendent telling that since he had been reported for the third time for unauthorized use of tobacco, he was being put on probation until the beginning of the next academic year.

That summer, things were happening in the Chesapeake Bay area that promised to change the science of warfare, and they dealt with aviation. In July Army-Navy bombing tests saw the sinking of a captured German destroyer, the light cruiser *Frankfort* and the battleship *Ostfriesland,* proving the vulnerability of naval craft to aerial attack. Dugan, now a third classman, was enjoying a summer cruise to Europe, aboard the *U.S.S. South Carolina.* The midshipmen were feted wherever they stopped in the ports of call. The Grand Hotel at Kristiania, Norway, and the Hotel Continental in Lisbon enjoyed the effervescent middies as they toured points of interest.

By the end of that summer, the battleship *Alabama* had been sunk in Chesapeake Bay by a 2,000 pound bomb. And as "Red" Dugan studied hard on the difficult curriculum, he was aware that the U.S. Army *Roma* made an initial flight November 15, 1921 at Langley Field, Virginia. The newspapers also recorded that summer that a new

bureau was formed to handle Aeronautics in the Navy, headed by Rear Admiral William A. Moffett. Like others with an interest in aviation, Dugan was shocked when on August 24, 1921, the British airship *R-38,* scheduled for delivery to the U.S. Navy as the *ZR-2* (Zeppelin Rigid Number 2), broke up during her trials over Hull, England. Forth-three lives were lost, including the nucleus of the Navy's pioneering airship program. General Edward Maitland-Maitland, who had crossed the Atlantic in the *R-34* in July of 1919, was lost in the crash and burning of the *ZR-2* in the Humber River. He was found still clutching the ballast toggles when he was pulled from the crumpled mass of girders, wires and fabric in the murky waters of the Humber. Cdr. Louis Maxfield, Naval Aviator No. 17, and the cream of the first generation of airship men were lost, but construction of the *ZR-1,* a 680-foot long rigid based on the captured German Zeppelin *L-49,* was commencing at the Naval Aircraft Factory, for assembly at Lakehurst. Delivery of the U.S. Navy's first helium-filled large rigid airship was still two years away.

Tragedy, part and parcel of life, occurred elsewhere which Dugan might have been aware of through his Navy contacts. In August, a charming New Yorker who had served as Assistant Secretary of the Navy and showed great promise as a rising politician was stricken with infantile paralysis at his summer home at Campobello, New Brunswick, Canada. His name: Franklin D. Roosevelt.

During his youngster year of 1921-22, "Red" Dugan picked up 35 demerits, about par for the course while getting accustomed to regimented life. Five demerits were for "skylarking" in ranks, which he admitted he deserved, and another five were for failing to observe restrictions to study hours. The latter infraction showed that the redhead with the determined jaw could spend long hours at books of a highly technical nature, even after hours. He helped a number of his friends reach an understanding of the Calculus which they had not had before receiving clarification from Jim Dugan.

Meanwhile, earlier that month, the U.S. Army Air Service on August 10, 1921 received a crated semi-rigid airship purchased from Italy for $165,000. The huge envelope for the 410-foot *Roma* was found upon inspection to be covered with mildew. Her six Ansaldo 450 horsepower engines had proved unreliable when test flown in

A view showing the rigid nose of the *Roma*, seen in a picture taken in mid-November of 1921, at Langley Field, Virginia. A semi-rigid airship, the *Roma's* only other internal framework was the triangular-shaped keel under the envelope. Besides 11 individual gas compartments, the ship had six air compartments.
John B. Mitchell, Director, Syms-Eaton Museum photo

Italy by Captain Dale Mabry and others of the Army Air Service acceptance team, but the plan was to substitute 400 h.p. Liberty engines as soon as possible. Inspection crews had to patch 184 holes in six of the ship's 11 compartments for holding the highly-flammable hydrogen used to provide lift. Using non-burning helium was out of the question. A thousand cubic feet of helium then cost $120; a like amount of hydrogen was only two dollars. The *Roma* had a strange box-kite like tail and utilized two rudder-wheels and one elevator wheel in the control car. There was little in her appearance to inspire enthusiasm for flying her, and it is unlikely that Midshipman James Dugan had any interest in the Army ship if he saw pictures of her in the newspapers. Certainly, he did not escape seeing the tragic news of her final flight of February 21, 1922. Carrying 45 men, seven of whom were civilians, on a flight from Langley Field to Hampton Roads, Virginia, the *Roma* departed after lunch and when airborne only a few minutes the nose of the ship began to press in. The crew worked on the air scoop, pushed a little air into the nose and thought the problem was solved.

From the Hampton Roads Naval Base, an observer, Lt. James Lawrence, noticed that the box kite rudder was tilted to the left, and the *Roma* was losing altitude. Further deterioration of the rudder was heralded to those aboard ship with three distinct vibrations of the ship. Travelling at more than 50 m.p.h., the nose kept failing and the rudder-elevator had broken. Nose down, she plowed helplessly into high-voltage wires at the Army Quartermaster Intermediate Depot, amid warehouses and railroad tracks. First Lt. Byron Burt, at the elevator wheel, found it would not respond. They cut nearby engines to idle, but forward engines were going at full speed. Sparks from the telephone pole wires set off three explosions of the hydrogen and a mass of flame shot into the air as the ship hit the ground, the burning envelope draping over the crew and the wires. Thirty-four men were killed, eight injured and three were uninjured, including among the latter Lt. Byron Burt. Held back by cable entangled around his legs, Burt fell on the ground several times until the cable broke and he emerged unscathed.

The *Roma* disaster caused the military to take a new look at using hydrogen. The U.S. Navy made plans to lower the cost of helium and use it in its own airship program. On December 7, 1922, LCdr. Zachary Lansdowne flew the blimp *C-7* from

Hampton Roads to Washington and return and successfully proved the desirability of using helium as the lifting agent.

In September of 1922 "Red" met a pretty brunette from Lexington, Kentucky, named Frances Lathrop Smith. She was an honor student, a talented writer like himself, and she was on the rifle team at the University of Kentucky. Together, they had much fun at proms and athletic events, often double-dating with a tall, serious midshipman who had a way with words—Hanson Baldwin. He had known Dugan from Baltimore. Baldwin would regale Jim and Frances with his knowledge of naval history. When he completed the course, he opined that he might be better off leaving the Service to follow his career of writing. Dugan was a fine descriptive writer too, but his scientific talent held him toward staying with the Navy for his career.

"I want to study to become a librarian," Frances said as they walked along the seawall with Baldwin and his "drag."

"If you keep your grades high," Jim said, "you'll probably make Phi Beta Kappa, Frances."

Baldwin, whose date was not particularly interested in their common bond of writing and scholarship, injected: "I suppose you'll keep a happy balance between the books and the horses."

Frances smiled. She knew only too well that her love of riding show horses in the land of the blue grass had to be controlled sufficiently for studying.

"Let's get back to the prom," Baldwin's date said. Grades were boring to her, as well as horses. The foursome went happily back to the ballroom at Bancroft Hall. "Red" and Frances, both 19, had their careers ahead of them. They were too young to want to be tied down to any responsibilities other than that of learning and reading and achieving as the Roaring Twenties Era began.

The tall redhead slowly adjusted to life in midshipman uniform. In October, he was caught hazing a plebe, a practice still continued despite efforts to wipe it out. Hazing was supposed to help the plebes respect authority, and "Red" Dugan had been on the receiving end himself. He was on pins and needles as to whether he would be severely disciplined or even bilged. When "Red" Dugan appeared before his superiors to answer the charge of gross unofficer-like bearing, the 20-year old lad stood erect and made every inch of his nearly 5 foot 11 inches count, although inwardly he was full of anxiety at the consequences, with Congress anxious to rid the Academy of hazing by mid-

After her first American flight in mid-November of 1921, the *Roma* lands, a broken propeller blade visible on the right forward engine. Her envelope was of three layers of rubberized cotton, which kept shape through the inflammable hydrogen used as lifting agent.
John B. Mitchell, Director, Syms-Eaton Museum photo

Aftermath of the collision of the *Roma* and telephone pole-held high voltage wires February 23, 1921.
Out of control due to a broken rudder and collapsed nose, the 410-foot long airship's remains smoulder
at the Army Quartermaster Depot near Hampton Roads, Virginia. Lt. William Riley's parachute, which failed
to deploy fully, is in the center foreground behind a sedan
John B. Mitchell, Director. Syms-Eaton Museum photo.

shipmen to sons of their constituents. The officer-in-charge read the account, then asked Dugan if he had anything to say to the charges as read.

"Sir, I was reprimanding Midshipman Trana for the condition of his uniform," Dugan said. "The charge relates that I walked 15 feet from my place in ranks to make the reprimand."

"That seems to be correct, Dugan," the officer said.

"I would like to point out respectfully, sir, that Midshipman Trana is number three in the rear rank of my squad. Therefore he was only one pace from my own position in ranks."

The officer and his associates realized that Dugan's point was well made. They conferred in hushed tones, then dismissed the charge on the basis of the error made in the charge, which cast doubt on the validity of the rest of the account as presented by Midshipman Trana.

Dugan saluted smartly, made an about face and as he headed back for Bancroft Hall, he breathed a sign of relief that he was off the hook. He vowed to be careful in his conduct—and if he did a bit of smoking now and then, he would be especially prudent that he wasn't caught at it.

From his father he had picked up the usefulness of finding a fallacy in an opponent's charges to swing the case to one's own advantage.

Thousands of miles westward, a naval officer who had preceded Dugan and Baldwin by a decade was commanding his destroyer in China. LCDR. Frank Carey McCord was 31 years old and because he was spending considerable time at sea, he had as yet not married. His superiors rated him highly, pointing out that he had conducted his ship from Chanchoo to Hankow without having a pilot aboard—an almost unprecedented occurrence.

In 1923, as Dugan became a second classman, McCord was commanding the *U.S.S. Charles Ausburn*. In McCord's fitness rating, he was granted 4.0—perfection—for professional ability. His superior said he showed "initiative, judgment and capability far beyond the average young of-ficer of his time."

Aviation achievements were coming to McCord's attention, even at the far-flung China Station. On May 2-3, 1923, news was received of the Army Air Service's making a first non-stop crossing of the United States in the Flying Fokker *T-2*. Lieutenants O. G. Kelly and J. A. Macready flew 2,520 miles from New York to San Diego in 26 hours and 50 minutes.

Other foreign news was carried in the papers for McCord and other naval personnel in China. One item that rated little space reported that on November 8-9, 1923 a radical politician named Adolph Hitler and General Ludendorff tried to set up a revolutionary government at Munich. The Putsch was easily suppressed by the Reichswehr and police. The short item which McCord read ended with the news that Hitler received sentence of five years detention in a fortress.

Back at Annapolis, Jim Dugan also kept up with news of foreign affairs. Since the Irish were well aware of the German families that were strong in number in his home city of Baltimore, he followed the goings on in Europe with more than passing interest. He had been a teenager during the war, but he remembered the Germans who engaged in spy activities and how many were caught by minute men organized to keep a watch on families suspected of being loyal to the Kaiser's cause.

Dugan stood midway in class ratings. His brother was graduated in 1922 and "Red" was determined to follow the same footsteps. Discipline in the early years was more of a problem than studies. "Red" gave promise of becoming a nonregulation officer as regards "spit and polish," but one who could be the most committed to any assignment in which he strongly believed. Of the senior Ferdinand Dugan's seven sons, four entered the services—Navy and Marines. Another son shipped as a common seaman and a brother was a general. A brother-in-law was an admiral. The Dugans had a capability for wearing the uniform of their country and serving it with honor.

Moored to the expeditionary mast at San Diego Naval Air Station, the *U.S.S. Shenandoah* is away from home base for 19 days as she makes a flight of 9,317 miles around the rim of the nation in October of 1924.
Official U.S. Navy photo.

CHAPTER TWO

Let the Twenties Roar

Like most other new Naval Academy graduates, Ensign Hammond James Dugan devoted the next several years to sea duty. He knew the thrill of speeding along in the black of a tropical night in a destroyer, keeping his hopes high that no other craft was close ahead. He also learned seamanship by instinct after many months in the sealanes, where with every ship sighted he had to quickly determine her bearing, course and speed and who had the right of way.

"Red" was out of the Academy only six months when the newspapers were filled with the court martial of Brig. Gen. William Mitchell, who until the March previous had been Assistant Chief of the Army Air Service. The precipitating factor that brought the outspoken Mitchell ultimately to a verdict of guilty of misconduct on December 17, 1925 was the wreck of the Navy's first U.S.-built large rigid airship, *U.S.S. Shenandoah.* Mitchell was a friend of LCdr. Zachary Lansdowne, the airship's captain. From the post to which Mitchell had been "exiled" in Texas, the young general called in newspaper reporters without permission of his superiors and accused those who sent Lansdowne to his death and the *Shenandoah* to fly over a handful of State Fairs on a rigid itinerary in thunderstorm season of being treasonous.

The tattered shards of fabric, twisted girders and dangling wires were still being taken by souvenir hunters when Mitchell's charges made the front pages. All America read Mitchell's claim that men were being killed by being sent out in airplanes and airships that were too old to be airworthy. (This was not the case of the *Shenandoah,* which broke apart in the air while trying to outrun two converging thunderstorms). Billy Mitchell shot from the hip, and much of what he said about the risks

of flying World War I surplus planes was true. But he had ignored the rules of the Service by contacting the press without the approval of his superior. He was suspended from duty for five years. Not finding the sentence acceptable, he resigned his commission.

Elsewhere, in Germany, Dr. Hugo Eckener was making an extensive circuit of lectures soliciting contributions from the rank and file to build a large commercial airship. The public responded to the man who earlier had written articles against Count von Zeppelin's airships by giving him two-and-a-half million marks. The German government came up with another one-and-a-half million. The design for the *LZ-127* called for it to have a capability to fly 6,214 miles with a payload of 33,069 pounds at 68 miles an hour. All Germany awaited completion of the new airship by July of 1928.

In the winter of 1926, an ailing Santos-Dumont appealed to the League of Nations for a ban on using flying machines in the event of war. The League's negative response was delivered to him in a Swiss sanatorium. By May of 1927, when the Lone Eagle, Charles A. Lindbergh, flew the Atlantic, the Aero Club of France invited Santos to the banquet given the young Army captain, who by virtue of his feat was jumped in rank immediately to a colonelcy. While the 25-year old Lindy was taken by the cruiser *Memphis* back to America by order of President Calvin Coolidge for a hero's welcome, the pioneering Brazilian was ill. At Valmont-sur-Territet sanatorium, he kept himself busy adapting a 17-pound engine producing a quarter horsepower to the sport of skiing.

Ballooning was garnering headlines in 1927 also,

Hydrogen-filled Navy balloon of the type used to train prospective airship officers at Lakehurst Naval Air Station, New Jersey. Judging from the clouds surrounding, the balloon will make a brisk flight. *National Air and Space Museum/Smithsonian Institute photo.*

16 Sky Ship – The Akron Era

and Lt. Thomas G. W. "Tex" Settle of the Navy set an official distance record for free balloon flight in a 19,000 cubic foot capacity balloon in February. Settle, a native of Washington, D.C. who picked up his nickname from having gone to the Naval Academy from Texas, covered 478 miles from Lakehurst to Lisbon Falls, Maine in 21 hours and 30 minutes. From 1927 to 1933 he was a stellar member of the Navy balloon teams, while instructing the ground school and lighter-than-air craft the last half of the 1920s. Besides flying in balloons and blimps, Settle was communications officer on the airships *Shenandoah* and *Los Angeles.*

The Navy kept its officers and men working hard for their salaries, and with all his other duties, "Tex" Settle also had charge of the parachute packers. He jumped regularly, both free-fall and regular low-altitude jumping. Two chutists would often be carried aloft on the wings of a DeHavilland biplane, since both could not fit into the cockpit, and the wiry Settle was no stranger to jumping along with those who were carried aloft to check their chute-packing skills.

For Ensign "Red" Dugan, the aviation achievements of 1927 became more and more enticing as he read of them in newspapers aboard ship. Less than a week after Lindbergh spanned the Atlantic, Lt. James H. Doolittle flew the first successful outside loop, on May 25, 1927.

Within a fortnight, on June 4, Clarence Chamberlin and a passenger named Levin made the first non-stop flight to Germany. Their Bellanca 15 with a Wright 200 h.p. engine covered the 3,911 miles in 43 hours and 49 minutes.

That same month, between June 20 and July 1, LCdr. Richard E. Byrd and Bert Acosta with two others aboard made a four-passenger flight from Roosevelt Field in New York to France—3,477 miles in 46 hours and six minutes. While they were flying eastward, two Army pilots on June 28-29 headed non-stop from California to Hawaii. Lieutenants Albert Hegenberger and L. J. Maitland in a twin-engined Fokker monoplane found the then elusive string of islands in a flight of 2,407 miles from Oakland to Wheeler Field, Honolulu, in 25 hours and 50 minutes. Their task was aided by directional beacons at San Francisco and on Maui, but it was still more difficult than finding the continent of Europe or Africa when flying eastward over the Atlantic.

A freakish incident happened the summer of 1927 to the *Los Angeles,* which due to the loss of the *Shenandoah* two years before was now the only rigid airship in active service with the Navy. Lt. "Tex" Settle was officer-of-the-deck and acting commanding officer in the control car as the airship was moored to the high mast at Lakehurst. Captain Rosendahl was on the ground while 25 officers and men aboard prepared the ship for flight.

The day was ending and a cool sea breeze was moving inland slowly as the ship rode at the 158 foot high mast. The cool easterly wind overtook the heated air over the land as the bow of the ship faced west. Settle's wife, Faye, was in a car driving a visitor to the railroad station and had stopped at the marine gate near the big hangar. She and her passenger, a consultant with whom "Tex" often met to discuss engineering matters, watched in amazement as the tail started climbing abruptly upwards.

A Navy photographer located nearby also saw the stern rising rapidly. He professionally put the camera to his eye and began snapping a series of pictures to record any unusual angles and attitudes that might develop.

The cold east wind was shoving the stern up both dynamically and statically. To bring the stern down, the crew was ordered from forward positions to the stern. The "galloping kilos" trying to get aft found themselves climbing vertically, firmly gripping girders to keep gravity from pulling them downward. Water ballast and fuel were dumped immediately, a considerable part of it drenching everyone below the point of fall as the ship kept going ever upward.

Lt. Settle was at the rudder station as the airship reached the top of the rise, his knees gripping the edge of a platform. An immense crashing of plastic dinnerware filled the air from the galley abaft the control car. Between his knees, Settle looked through the forward window at the ground 200 feet below—the bow was 158 feet above ground and the car was still farther from the bow.

Some of the crew felt the nose would collapse, and the airship would cave in over it. Pausing a second at the top, at 87 degrees from vertical, the LA appeared to wait as if for applause. Then her tail descended slowly, belly facing the surface, and in a few seconds her bow was facing the sea breeze that had helped her do her trick.

Outside of some holes in the cover from falling

Ground handling crew aboard the aircraft carrier *U.S.S. Saratoga* holds line toggles as the *U.S.S. Los Angeles* lands aboard ship January 27, 1928. Note lines fastened to either side of the carrier to aid in steadying the airship, whose propellers keep her headed into the wind.
Official U.S. Navy photo

objects, no structural damage occurred. No one was injured. It was a plus for airships—there were no airplanes that could do a standing outboard loop, after all.

Rosendahl commandeered the Navy photographer's pictures so there would be no adverse publicity. Since there was no damage nor injury, the press ignored the event. The airshipmen felt it was a great testimonial to the rugged design of the German-built LA, and there the story rested.

Ballooning earning its share of headlines that were not all of a positive nature. On a bleak November day in 1927, the Army's Captain Hawthorne Gray took off from Scott Field, Illinois in Army balloon *S-80-241* as America's first stratosphere flier. The barograph they recovered along with his body in the basket, near Sparta, Tennessee, indicated he had ascended eight miles above earth. An investigation found that he ran out of oxygen and had not delubricated his clock. After arriving at 42,470 feet, he valved for descent, but he died on the way down. Gray had successfully flown the same balloon to that altitude earlier.

That same year a design competition was held for the construction of two large airships for the U.S. Navy. Goodyear-Zeppelin Corp. at Akron and several serious entries competed. The American Brown-Boveri Electric Corporation did propose to design and build the airships at a lower cost. But when the design Project 1 was judged the next year, the Goodyear-Zeppelin people won. As called for by the Navy, the new ships would have engines fully enclosed in the structure of the airships, possible only because helium would be the lifting agent. Above each engine room would be five water recovery condensers, one above the other, flush with the hull. Twelve enormous gas cells would be the helium containers in each ship.

In 1928 an ailing Alberto Santos-Dumont took passage on the ocean liner *Cap Arcona* for a triumphant trip from Europe to his native land. While the liner was in sight of the harbor at Rio de Janeiro a large Junkers flying boat flew low over the wave-tops to meet the ship. Turning to meet the liner, a wing tip went into the water and there was an explosion of spray. Half-a-dozen of the nation's top professors and intellectuals were killed. Grief-stricken, Santos-Dumont had the sponsors cancel the welcome. He went out with the salvage boat until all were recovered. The mishap drove him to thoughts of suicide. When he re-

turned to Paris, a sympathetic nation made him a member of the Legion of Honour for his contributions to aviation.

Hammond James Dugan had been promoted to Lieutenant (junior grade) in October 1927 and six months later he was ordered to report to Lakehurst Naval Air Station for duty under instruction in Lighter-Than-Air craft.

On that April Fool's Day of 1928 when Jim Dugan reported for duty with other hand-picked volunteers there was no time for Tomfoolery. Only a small percentage of those who responded to the call for LTA volunteers were selected. The officer of the day told the small group of new arrivals they could take several days to move their things into the Bachelor Officers Quarters, check out flight gear and get acquainted with the station. Dugan and the rest were amazed at the sheer size of the giant airship dock. Hangar Number One, and its sliding doors, each weighing 1,200 tons.

Dugan was happy to learn that one of his instructors would be Lt. "Tex" Settle, winner of numerous balloon races as a representative of the U.S. Navy. The day soon arrived when he and others were lined up before the dark complected aeronaut, who outlined the course for them.

"You'll have three weeks of ground school," Settle said. "This will be followed by seven flights in free balloons—one of them a solo for more than an hour. Then you'll have ten flights in kite balloons. After this, if you pass each step along the way, we'll teach you to fly blimps. Finally, you'll get time aboard a rigid airship, the *Los Angeles.*"

Dugan learned from Settle that he would have a number of different instructors, but "Tex" would be with them as the instructors rotated among their charges. Ground school, covering airship structures and materials, airship engines, aerodynamics, aerostatics and airmanship, went by quickly.

Finally the day came which Red Dugan and his fellow students had eagerly awaited. The thrill of which there was none greater was about to be theirs. The balloon basket of a 35,000 cubic foot capacity balloon was carried bodily by ground handlers to a clear spot for takeoff. The balloon was weighed off a trifle light. Lt. "Tex" Settle tested the valve for releasing helium by giving a short pull on the valve cord. Then the seven men rose without a sound. There was no vibration. Only absolute calm. Dugan's first flight on the wings of the wind carried him and his companions silently

U.S.S. Los Angeles (ZR-3) **in flight with Admiral William Moffett aboard, his flag flying.**
Official U.S. Navy photo.

Free-ballooning was a requirement in the training of airship pilots as late as 1957.

Official U.S. Navy photo

over the vast pine forests, which Lt. Settle called "the Boondocks." The patches of open ground, cranberry bogs and marshes next sped by on frictionless bearings as the balloon was wafted along by an easterly wind.

Since the ocean was but 15 miles to the east, there were no ascensions unless the winds would blow them inland. The new aeronauts learned that the sun's rays heat the land unequally. The heated portions of the land cause up currents and cooler areas with down-drafts,which make the balloonist work fast to keep clear of the trees without expending ballast unnecessarily.

Of one of those early balloon flights, Dugan later wrote both Hanson Baldwin, who was with the *Baltimore Sun* then, and Frances Lathrop Smith, his sweetheart in Kentucky, of his training. Red explained that in his first balloon there was a panel in the upper part which is ripped off on landing by pulling a cord in the basket. Carrier pigeons also were carried aboard to bear messages back to the station. One student was making certain a pigeon was secure when the balloon hit turbulence. The student snatched for support and his hand grabbed the rip cord. He caught himself, but erroneously figured he had pulled the rip panel, since a downdraft was carrying the balloon down a full thousand feet, surprising to the student officer and disgusting to the pilot.

On one of the other early student flights, the instructor was teaching his half-dozen neophytes that if the balloon starts to drop because it is temporarily heavy, the pilot tosses out a handful or two of sand. The balloon later became heavy and went down to about a hundred feet above a spiked green tree. Alarmed, the student instead of dropping a handful of sand at the command to "Drop ballast," dropped over the side an entire bag of sand, weighing thirty-five pounds. The balloon jerked up to 4,000 feet in a trice. The student learned immediately how small quantities of ballast can affect the balloon.

The students learned to attempt landings near a railroad, where the balloon could be packed after deflation and shipped back to Lakehurst. From the class ahead of them, they learned of the delights of night flight. Fantastic journeys, they were told, above lighted peaks and towers, across sparkling lakes and meandering rivers until dawn paints its vivid picture to the east.

Red Dugan was 25 years old as his LTA schooling began. He began writing fluidly to the girl he had known since both were 19 years old and he was a third classman at the Academy. Looking at the long, detailed curriculum, he wrote jestingly to the brunette in Kentucky: "My particular wings have many miles to fly before lighting upon my manly bosom." He also had time for introspection. He felt that the duty he had asked for would mean the absolute end of what he enjoyed most—reading selectively. But he had made his decision. It must be all aviation, or none. He decided to put his whole soul into airships. Should fortune favor him and grant him his wings of gold, he would then try to get a postgraduate course in aeronautical construction. Dugan believed there was a big future for dirigibles. His only personal fear was that he would have to study so hard that his eyes, already giving signs of strain, would weaken so that he wouldn't measure up physically.

Having just have a physical exam where he was barely able to read the eye chart, he planned to somehow know the chart beforehand in time for the next physical.

Frances Smith kept Red enlightened of her activities, particularly her participation in horse shows. She also was studying to be a librarian. She expressed an uneasiness that he was taking on a hazardous part of the Service. He assured her that LTA was too highly developed for accidents to occur—the only accidents of note at the station were those happening in automobiles. One anecdote had Cdr. Joseph P. "Swifty" Norfleet one time *Shenandoah* navigator, driving into the base while reading *The Wall Street Journal.* He became engrossed in one report and he and the car were interrupted by a tree. The *Journal* under his arm, "Swifty" limped into his office and ordered a subordinate matter-of-factly to take the wrecked car to a garage.

Much of Dugan's time was spent not in flying but in studying. He considered that studying aerostatics and a dozen other subjects at Lakehurst made the Naval Academy like a kindergarten.

Six weeks after he had first reported at Lakehurst, Red Dugan went on his first overnight balloon hop. Once aloft and borne westward, the only witnesses to the silent passage of the creature in the black of night were barking dogs and squalling chickens. Nobody slept in the basket, what with the crunching of the wicker home as anyone moved around, and the excitement of the flight.

N2Y-1 approaching the *U.S.S. Los Angeles* to hook on trapeze in August of 1931.
Official U.S. Navy photograph.

Occasionally, they would yell down for their position.

"Where are we?" came the cry.

"You're in the United States!" came the reply.

"C'mon down for breakfast," somehow below invited.

"What are you having this morning?" an aeronaut asked.

Then those on the ground would yell up what was on the bill of fare. The hungry Navy balloonists had learned enough to wait for the invitation which carried the most appetizing breakfast before they would make their landing.

They were about to land in response to one particularly promising invitation of eggs, pancakes and sausage when they discovered the rip cord had been cemented on too long and was holding firmly. Four students put their weight on the rip cord. The panel didn't budge. Finally they missed the farm where they intended to land, and after they "unstuck" the rip panel to a degree, the seven in the basket were smashed through a row of trees. The basket wound up against a tree, the empty balloon draped over the limbs and looking like a sick elephant. It turned out they were over the State Prison Farm near Norristown, Pennsylvania. Thirty convicts were there to assist with the landing, while rain started coming down. The field was completely muddy by the time they had secured the equipment. The warden took the students to the jail in Norristown and gave them striped prison clothes while their wet flight uniforms dried out. The balloonists dined at the local Young Men's Christian Association, and the pork upset their stomachs to a man.

Later overnight flights were more rewarding, when delicious breakfasts brought more suitable endings to their passage through the night.

By the end of May 1928 Frances Smith was planning a trip abroad. "Red" had been to Scotland on his midshipman cruises, so he told her to be sure and see the only real castle he remembered, which was in Edinburgh—stuck up high on the edge of a huge rock. He didn't know whether he could see her off in New York, even though it was so close by Lakehurst. He explained to her that no one knew whether or not he could have leave over a weekend because if the weather permitted, the airship *Los Angeles* would be sent out. All hands had to be present to take the big ship out and bring her back in, and some of the student officers

would be given a ride on the airship as part of their training.

A balloon of the second flight of trainees exploded loudly as they were deflating it on the ground about this time. The friction from removing the valve created a spark which set off the hydrogen. Dugan was only several yards away, attaching a message to one of his own flight's pigeons. Fortunately, no one was hurt. It was the first time it had happened at the station. "Red" Dugan hoped it would be the last.

On August 11, 1928, Frances Smith sailed for Europe on the *Homeric*. The night she sailed, Red Dugan was only a half-mile away from her. He was on watch in one of the engine cars of the *Los Angeles* as it overflew the Hudson river.

Looking down as the ocean liner headed out to sea, Red felt like he was hanging in space with the world laid out below. The millions of twinkling lights added to the glitter of the liner's sailing. Then the LA went on to Newport, and an hour before dawn she moored to the converted oil-tender, *Patoka.*

On the return flight down the coast Dugan was on watch. Every time he sighted a ship he experienced a hundred thrills. It was his first experience at sighting ships at sea without having to bother whether there was danger of collision or who had the right-of-way.

With Frances Smith touring Europe, Dugan concentrated on the study of aerostatics, meteorology and numerous other courses designed to train the Lighter-Than-Air pilot. The wings he hoped to earn were identical with those worn by Heavier-Than-Air pilots. The only difference between the two categories of airmen were that the LTA pilots when qualified bore in parenthesis after their designation as pilot (airship). Receiving cards and letters from Frances from the continent was the only respite he had from the arduous course, even though he was in love with flying. The kite balloons, which looked like giant boxing gloves and had the basket tethered to the land or to a ship in service held no particular thrill for him. He liked free-ballooning, and he champed at the bit to take another ride in the *Los Angeles,* which was not allowed to fly unless the weather was promising. Since the loss of the *Shenandoah* three years earlier, the Navy did not want to chance losing its only remaining large rigid airship.

On September 7, 1928, Dugan again was one of

Hook-on test with low hook-on device on *N2Y-1* plane. August 1931.
Official U.S. Navy photo

the students selected to make a local flight on the *Los Angeles*. The ship left at sunset, but shortly after they left a summer thunderstorm broke over Lakehurst. Instead of landing into disaster, with the gusts, updrafts and downdrafts of such a storm, the *Los Angeles* flew up and down the Atlantic coast until early morning. By 4 a.m. Jim Dugan was looking down on New York City as the LA headed up the Hudson. How wonderful the low level view was to the young lieutenant junior grade, getting another cruise on a large rigid. The ship of the sky passed West Point, Poughkeepsie, Albany and then penetrated the mountain passes to Lake George, whose waters sparkled from the sunlight like diamonds.

Circling, the airship then flew over Saratoga Springs and Schenectady. Dugan went into the control room—the estate of "Aridalia" of Frances Smith's aunt and uncle was only five miles away now. There was a possibility that she might have returned from Europe already. Visibility was 30 miles, and although he was but a student officer, he asserted himself to borrow a pair of binoculars from the navigator. They were over a landmark called Pond Eddy on the Delaware River. Dugan was dismayed when he could not find the valley in which the estate was located since it was abeam of the airship's course. He vowed someday when he became qualified in the J-blimps to start out early, follow the Delaware river to that Landmark and reach "Aridalia." He figured it would take four hours from Lakehurst if the weather were ideal. How proud he would be to wave down to Frances, if she were at "Aridalia." As it turned out, she was not coming back until mid-September; so he had to describe the trip via letter instead of waving to her from a thousand feet.

A month later, on October 8, Jim Dugan had another memorable overnight free balloon flight. With five other students and an instructor, he piled into the basket already loaded with instruments, maps, pigeons, food and a gallon jug of coffee. Up they rose into the faint red afterglow. The night was perfect, not even a cloud. The earth slid quietly below in an endless pattern of blacks and lighter blacks, which changed to silver as the rising moon took charge. The aeronauts could hear the leaves rustling in the trees, deer snorting and scampering through the woods.

"Red" Dugan marvelled at the music of running water clearly heard in the balloon, and the sound of people talking below. From time to time, dogs seeing the aluminum-colored bag would set up a mournful howl. Chickens cackled and flapped their wings to escape from the terrifying hulk overhead— was it some super-gigantic hog?

Occasionally over the mountains they ran into a down current. They dropped sand ballast and rose again. After another downdraft, they just barely cleared the roof of a farmhouse—Dugan could have touched it by reaching down with his hand. The balloon scraped through trees nearby, the farmer's dog started howling and the lights went on in the house. The seven balloonists sat down in the bottom of the basket and prayed the farmer wouldn't get out his shotgun and blast away at the big silvery ball some fifty feet above his land in the middle of the night.

Once again Dugan realized by the compass course that the wind was taking them toward "Aridalia." But at Middletown, Delaware around 3:30 a.m. the wind shifted and they headed southward. He curled up to sleep on top of the sand bags, but when any of them moved the basket creaked.

With the rising sun, people began showing themselves below. They landed at one farm and tethered the balloon. To the farmer—who provided pancakes, butter, maple syrup, fried ham and coffee— they gave a short flight as his reward. The farmer was shaking like a leaf but tickled to death. The wind was still good, so they put off again, landing next in a school yard.

The children nearly went wild as Dugan and his friends touched down.

"We were just starting arithmetic class," one boy yelled. "Hot dog!"

After telling the children about their flight, the balloonists deflated the bag and had it shipped back to Lakehurst with them from the nearby railroad station.

Dugan had completed his motorless flight training, and now was to learn how to fly the J-Class blimps. These were a tenth the size of the *Los Angeles*. Part of the training would see him flying low over the beaches, waving to the bathing beauties some 50 feet down and to the side of the blimp's overwater path. Skimming along over the breakers in his blimp, Dugan knew that if it ever dropped to the wave tops the car would be torn completely off the bag. By merely hitting the ocean, the blimp's car could be overturned. However, the instructor with him in the control car was a married man with two children. "Red" figured

Above, Two U.S. Navy officers pause while seeing that the *Graf Zeppelin* is provisioned at Mines Field, San Diego, in preparation for the last leg of her round-the-world flight in 1929. At left is Lt. T.G.W. "Tex" Settle, who made arrangements for helium, gasoline, oil and food and obtained the necessary ground crew. The taller officer is Lt. (jg) Karl Lange, his assistant. At left, the *Graf* being docked. *Worthington Collection, EAA Aviation Museum photo.*
At left, the *Graf* being docked. *National Air and Space Museum photo.*

there was little risk involved in the low-level flight with a family man aboard. Still, the brisk wind was shipping the waves in toward shore at an angle with possibly a strong current heading out to sea in places. He dismissed the thought of making any mistakes on the elevator wheel that would bring them any closer to the white foam, blowing into mist like the manes of charging white horses.

In October the *Graf Zeppelin, LZ-127,* made her first round-trip Atlantic crossing to Lakehurst. Cdr. Charles E. Rosendahl made the westward crossing. Cdr. Maury Pierce, and Lieutenants "Tex" Settle and Charles Bauch were on the eastward voyage. On the trip over from Germany a large piece of fabric ripped off of a horizontal fin. Dr. Hugo Eckener's son and assistants replaced the covering with table cloths so the ship would not be vulnerable in further turbulent weather.

The fall of 1928 turned into winter and in the clear weather devoid of the haze of summer flying, Dugan honed his skill at flying blimps. It took a special talent to anticipate the upward and downward movements, and Dugan proved to have sensitive hands indeed.

With what little time he had for reading other than the textbooks dealing with the LTA course, Jim Dugan worked in a few intellectual books from time to time, even though it didn't help his eyes to do too much reading. He enjoyed wrestling with Bertrand Russell's interpretations of relativity and atomic structures which often retired him at the end of an evening mentally *hors de combat.* His library also included relaxation reading in the forms of books like "Strange Interlude" and "Ultima Thule."

Dugan also read the newspapers and kept up with aviation milestones. As 1929 came in, he was enthralled by the unofficial endurance record for refueled airplane flight set by Major Carl Spaatz and Captain Ira Eaker. Their Fokker *C2-3* with a Wright 220 engine stayed aloft over Los Angeles Airport for 150 hours and 40 minutes. He hoped the world would remember that an airship could stay flying for a like period carrying a much greater payload and could rest her engines in any combination under all but the most severe weather conditions.

On February 7, 1929, Jim Dugan celebrated his twenty-sixth birthday. Reflecting to one of his fellow student officers, he mused that at that age Alexander the Great had conquered his world. Lindbergh had flown the ocean. "Red" had the

talent to be a very good writer, and sometimes he would dream of the writing he would like to do. His lack of time to write, when he had the urge to do so made him feel worthless at times. Then he would dismiss the negative thoughts and bury himself in some technical tome dealing with lighter-than-air flying.

His birthday did hold some promise in that he needed only a solo check ride and two solos in the J-Class blimp to qualify as a non-rigid airship handler—even though he might not conquer the world as early in life as Alexander. Early on that birthday his name was not on the list to fly. But at lunch, Dugan was told to be ready to go up at one o'clock in the afternoon. As he climbed into the control car, he was told that he must make a good landing, and if so, a second solo would be made the next day. Without any trouble, Dugan made the good landing and at 3:30 p.m. he qualified as a non-rigid airship handler. Now all he needed were a hundred more hours in the *Los Angeles.* To earn his wings he would also qualify in machine guns and bombing and pass a final written and oral exam.

All the headlines of the day were not of aviation. A week after Dugan soloed in blimps, the February 14th St. Valentine's Day Massacre took place in Chicago. March came and with it Lt. (jg) H. J. Dugan, U.S.N., had a new Commander-in-Chief, Herbert Clark Hoover. The economy of the country was having difficult days and Hoover based his thinking on his experience as Secretary of Commerce under both Presidents Harding and Coolidge. Hoover believed that in many areas where federal help could solve the problem, the federal government had no power to act.

"Red" Dugan kept abreast of developments in his field as well as a wary eye on the nation's economy. Any reduction in the national defense appropriation or threats of reducing the salaries of men in uniform hurt him and his fellows. A metal-clad blimp was being manufactured for the first time, and February 1929 had seen the two halves of the hull of the promising *ZMC-2* joined. Everyone at Lakehurst was vitally interested in this new "tin blimp" which would one day be flown to the big Hangar Number One, if the Navy found her acceptable.

The March winds wrecked a *J-3* and a *J-4* blimp in Washington. An Army blimp crashed into the trees near the big hangar while visiting Lakehurst landing with a bone-shaking crunch from nearly as

U.S.S. Los Angeles and the U.S. Navy blinps *J-2* (left) and the Metalclad *ZMC-2*, the latter flown
by Lt. Hammond J. Dugan as captain, overfly the *Raleigh* during maneuvers off Atlantic City October
11, 1930.
Official U.S. Navy photo.

high as the Washington Monument. Somehow, the three men aboard escaped without serious injury.

While Jim Dugan was getting his hundred hours aboard the *Los Angeles,* one particular flight was one not soon forgotten. The LA was a hundred miles from shore, looking for a lost patrol plane. The wind from the west was blowing so hard that for seven hours the airship stayed over the same quarter of ocean. They had been fighting head-winds for a total of twelve hours and fuel was getting alarmingly low. Dugan had eaten the last slice of bread and thoughts entered his mind of free-ballooning across the Atlantic in the airship without any fuel. Arising after sleeping to go on watch, Dugan could see the lights of Atlantic City finally. They landed with only two hours of fuel remaining.

What a blow to LTA had the wind continued, Dugan thought. The loss of the *Shenandoah* had retarded progress for a decade. If the LA were lost, it would probably take a generation to recover. What the movement needed now were a few more successful trans-Atlantic flights to prove to the world the usefulness of airships.

May of 1929 brought with it the sweet smell of spring but did nothing toward improving the depression in the economy toward which the nation was moving inexorably. Newspaper stories of aviation achievements at least took the minds of the public off their plight, even if for but a short time. May 4, 1929 witnessed the finish of the National Balloon Race. Lt. "Tex" Settle and Ensign Wilfred Bushnell of the Navy won with a 925-mile flight from Pittsburgh to Savage Harbor, Prince Edward Island.

On May 16 the *Graf Zeppelin* aborted its trip to South America when four out of her five engine units failed. Newly installed clutches had caused severe vibrations and the steel crank-shafts of the engines succumbed to fatigue. The *Graf,* being a commercial vessel of the skies, was being flown wisely by men with several decades experience. Some of the Germans had been with the half-dozen airships which flew all over Germany between 1911-14 and carried some 35,000 passengers for *Delag,* the world's first airline. The men who flew the *Graf* flew her with caution. They didn't press her into heavy weather situations, but avoided them.

The *Graf* made a round trip every two weeks, carrying 20 tons of cargo and 20 passengers. The westerly trip from Frederichshafen to Pernam-

bunco required three days and the easterly crossing took just under four days. She spent only four days out of each two weeks in the hangar. There were four captains who flew her safely for a life-time of 7 years: Ernst Lehmann, Hans Fleming, Hans von Schiller and Anton Wittemann. Dr. Hugo Eckener, who had written many articles *against* the airship before he joined up with the aging Count Zeppelin, was now "Mr. Airship" to a world that worshipped his skill in offering safe over-ocean flight.

May 20, 1929 was a halcyon day for Lt. (jg) Jim Dugan at Lakehurst. The wings which he said had many miles to fly before being pinned to his chest finally had flown the prescribed number of hours and he had passed the flight and oral exams. Dugan simultaneously was given his wings of gold and named a flight instructor. When he wasn't busy participating in numerous experiments dealing with the mechanical handling of the *Los Angeles,* he relaxed as athletic officer—which sometimes left him bone tired by the time for sleep came in the Bachelor Officers Quarters.

Dugan soon received word that he had been selected to go to Detroit on temporary duty in connection with the turning over of the metalclad blimp *ZMC-2* (Zeppelin Metal Clad number two). About July 1st, he would be on duty as test pilot and assistant inspector with the manufacturers.

Dugan worried about his physical, necessary to permit him to take the challenging duty at Detroit or continue flying of any sort, since he knew he had what the ophthalmologists termed variable hyperforia. With his extensive studying and love for reading, he had learned that his right eye did most of the work while the other one goldbricked. He was smart enough to know the extent of his defect as related to his problem by talking with the medics. He had figured how to compensate in taking the exam so that his problem was not so pronounced that he would fail it.

However, as he sat taking the eye exam, he was nervous about passing the test. He looked through a gadget with a pair of barrels, one side without glass and two lenses in the other—one astigmatic, and rotated by thumb screws. Working with a small dot of light at the other end of the room, manipulation of the astigmatic lens changed the dot to a horizontal streak of light. The idea was to turn the thumb screw until the streak passed through the dot. Unfortunately Dugan overextended to correct the defect so that the line and the dot came out

Lasting for more than a decade, the metalclad blimp *ZMC-2* shows her unique tail configuration. First captain of the "tin ship" was Lt. (jg) Hammond James Dugan. Developmental ship was to find whether aluminum clad airships would be more suitable than fabric covered airships, with a view to making large rigids of the new metal "alclad".
Official U.S. Navy photo

side by side instead. The doctor was sympathetic and patted Dugan on the shoulder.

"Too much flying, Lieutenant," he said. "Rest your eyes over the weekend and come see me Monday."

Dugan stayed away from the books. When he returned he estimated for his defect practically perfectly and passed. The Navy doctor did give him the name of a specialist in New York City in the event he wished outside help with his variable hyperforia, and Dugan planned to visit the civilian doctor as soon as he could.

July found Dugan on board in Detroit, observing completion of the metalclad blimp. While boning up on all the details of the *ZMC-2*, he did note by the newspapers that July 17 a Dr. Robert Goddard at Auburn, Massachusetts had fired an eleven-foot rocket carrying a small camera and a barometer. Both were recovered intact. He knew this was basic research for the future, but the *ZMC-2* was research of a more immediate nature since if successful it indicated that full-size airships could have long-lasting outer covering instead of cotton, and instead of a number of gas cells the entire interior could be filled with the helium which would stay airtight.

Dugan quickly made friends with the chief flight instructor on duty at the Naval Reserve Heavier-Than-Air unit hangar at the same airport at Grosse Isle. The instructor was fascinated by the metalclad being constructed in the neighboring hangar. Dugan was given a half-hour airplane flight and from 2,000 feet the HTA officer performed a few aerobatics which left Dugan breathless and tied him in knots against the seat as the forces of gravity made their presence known. He quickly learned to love the plane rides. Every Saturday and Sunday afternoon, weather permitting, the two went up and Dugan was given flying lessons that were quite different than flying balloons, blimps and airships. As time went on, he hoped the commanding officer would risk a plane and let him make a solo flight.

The inflation of the *ZMC-2* was not running exactly on schedule and now wouldn't take place until August 10. Dugan then set about knowing every bolt and rivet in the ship before it would leave for Lakehurst. To some of the questions of manufacture and design, he found he had to assume his most intelligent expression and say "good" or "bad," depending on the tone of the voice of the questioner. He wrote jestingly to

Frances Smith that if she heard of "the ship cracking up on the first flight, you will know just where the fault lay."

Dugan studied until about ten o'clock every night, and while waiting for the final stages of manufacture to be concluded on the *ZMC-2* he looked forward to his weekend flying with the HTA instructor. On July 24, he was shown how to land the aircraft. He also was having difficulty keeping the left wing level with the right, but soon he became accustomed to the effect of torque from the propeller which on takeoff particularly called for opposite rudder to bring the left wing up. Dugan hoped his flying wasn't going to interfere with his studies about the tin ship.

Somehow the manufacturer's people got the schedule back on the track and on August 5 they finished inflation and weighed the ship off. It was a Saturday night, and Dugan had been making landings in the airplane that afternoon to qualify for soloing. Carl Fritchie, president of the Aircraft Development Company, held a dinner to celebrate the event. Dugan listened intently as the gray-haired developer spoke.

"It has taken us five years and three-quarters of a million dollars to build the *ZMC-2*" he said. "Our next ship will be 12 or 15 times the present size—two hundred thousand cubic feet capacity. She will go a hundred miles an hour instead of only sixty."

Members of the press were present, as well as her designer, Ralph Upson. Upson explained to them after the dinner how the aluminum alloy, called alclad, was riveted to twelve circular frames.

"She's built roughly like the back of a fish," Upson told the newsmen. "The dozen frames are stiffened by wires placed diametrically across the hull's interior."

Each person attending the dinner was presented with a handsome hardbound book profusely illustrated and covering the progress in the making of the *ZMC-2*. A sample piece of the alclad material was tipped into the book.

On August 8, Dugan was sent to Cleveland in connection with landing and servicing the *Los Angeles,* on her arrival for the Air Races between August 24 and September 1. He did not look forward to breaking in a bunch of green men to be a landing party, and he was not sure whether he would be returned to duty at Lakehurst or returned to the *ZMC-2* for the flight to the station.

After spending several days briefing the landing

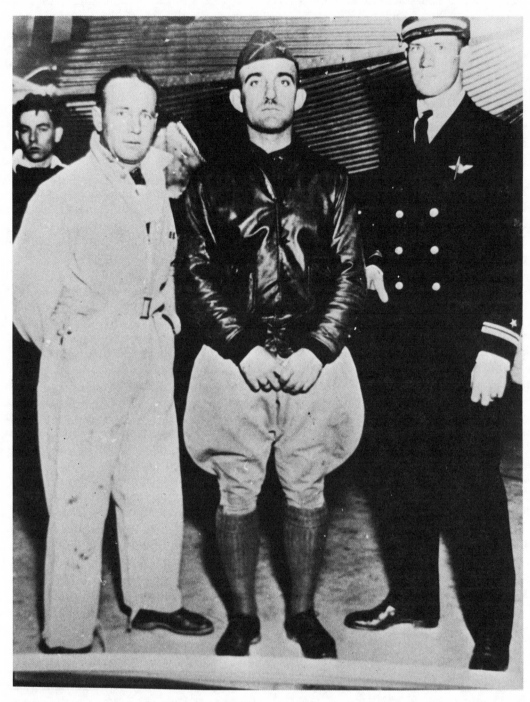

Crew of the *ZMC-2* prior to the first flight of the "tin ship" from Detroit to Lakehurst, N. J. From left: Sgt. Joe Bishop, Captain William Kepner, U.S. Army Air Service, and Lt. (jg) H. J. "Red" Dugan, U.S.N., who was given command when the blimp arrived at the Naval Air Station.
"Dugan Letters" Maryland Historical Society photo

party, Dugan was sent back to Grosse Isle and the *ZMC-2*.

On August 17 Dugan felt as if he were on cloud nine. He received two letters and a postcard from Frances and he also met his contemporary and everyone's idol, Col. Charles A. Lindbergh. Young Lindy had flown in to see the tin ship. Dugan was so honored to shake Lindbergh's hand he could think of nothing to say other than, "Pleased to meet you sir."

Lighter-Than-Air was making headlines throughout the month of August, since the *Graf Zeppelin* started her round the world flight on the first. The Hearst newspapers and the German press defrayed half the cost. Passenger tickets were sold and payments from stamp collectors also helped. The postcards and envelopes franked with commemorative stamps or struck with special cachets were in great demand. The *Graf* carried 63 persons, including LCdr. Charles E. Rosendahl as the U.S. Naval observer. Her progress was eagerly watched in the papers by the public. She flew across Berlin, East Prussia, the Baltic States, Siberia and landed near Tokyo August 19. She made Los Angeles, and a few days later was docked safely at Lakehurst.

Tuesday, August 20, 1929, found Lt. Jim Dugan dashing off a letter in the hangar at Grosse Isle to his sweetheart, Frances Smith. The porky little blimp had been up twice and Dugan was still a bridesmaid regarding flying her or in her. Two more senior officers of the Navy acceptance board had gone on the early flights.

The *ZMC-2* had less than a 3-to-1 fineness range—actually 2.83 to 1, which made it tend to be slightly unstable longitudinally. The Aircraft Development Company had made her for a crew of three, but four were aboard on the first flight as well as the second, to accommodate those with a special interest in her.

That same day he had learned that he was indeed to make the flight in the *ZMC-2* to Lakehurst.

"What do they intend to do with it?" Dugan asked one of the company spokesmen.

"It is to be given to you," the man replied.

"What'll I do with it?" Dugan asked making conversation.

"Probably crack it up" came the joking reply.

An experienced Army airship pilot, Capt. William E. Kepner, made the test flights. The twin-engine blimp was seven inches short of being 150 feet long and she was 52 feet in diameter at her thickest part. Big and beefy Lt. Charles E. Bauch watched the test flight from the ground along with Dugan. Bauch had walked safely away from the *Shenandoah's* crash four years earlier. He was attached to the *Los Angeles* now, but was on hand as an experienced blimp pilot if they needed one with more experience than Dugan.

A light breeze blew across the field at 6:45 p.m. as the *ZMC-2* rose lightly from the broad flying field outside her hangar, Kepner at the controls. With her unique eight fins, she looked like a cute little flying pig. She did not toss but pursued a steady course into the setting sun, which reflected from its polished metal hull. This was her second flight—she had been up for 40 minutes the day before. Now on August 20, she began her 30 hour test.

"She's only two-thirds the size of the largest of the LA's gas cells." Bauch mused as Dugan addressed his envelope for the letter to Frances.

"She's chubby," said Dugan, "but being pleasingly plump should make her more efficient in the air than the thinner zeppelins, I should think."

"You'll know more after you've had a chance to wring her out, 'Red'," said Bauch.

"There are surely to be arguments for and against the metalclads" Dugan said. "At least she has been built and flown successfully; so those who said she was a failure have been proven wrong already."

"Soon you'll have her among the other training and experimental ships at Lakehurst, and we'll know more about her," Bauch said.

The *ZMC-2* returned and they watched her brought to a nice landing by Capt. Kepner. Commander Garland Fulton and Lt. C. V. S. Knox, the Navy inspector, alighted with pleased looks on their faces. Dugan as he looked at the stern of the new blimp felt it looked like a pin cushion as well as a cute piglet. He like all the other LTA men had heard the jibes about being "nursemaid to a bloated sausage" or "joy-riding in a bucket hanging from a bag." Still, the HTA men who tossed out those rejoinders were those who never had experienced the joys of buoyant flight, where to stop an engine did not spell immediate disaster but meant saving gas and provided a leisurely time to survey the scene around you.

The evening of September 11, Red Dugan sent a Western Union wire to Frances Smith at 2255 Limestone Lexington, Kentucky. It read: "Got away tonight. Cheerio. Red."

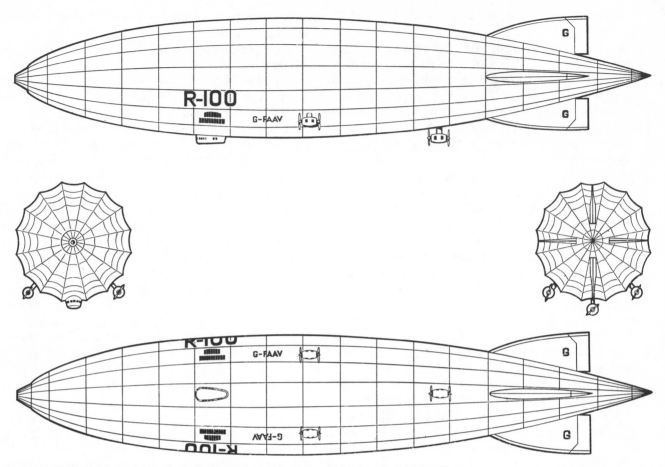

The *R-100*, of 5 million cubic foot displacement, was 709 feet long and 133 feet in diameter. She cruised at 71 m.p.h. with six Rolls-Royce Condor petrol engines. She was launched December 16, 1929, and in 1930 flew from England to Canada and return carrying 42 persons. Designer Dr. B. N. Wallis was later famous for his geodetic construction of the Vickers Wellington bomber.

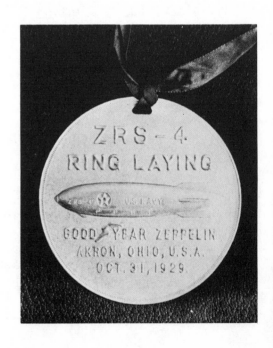

Souvenir of the *ZRS-4* ring laying October 31, 1929.
The airship later was christened the *U.S.S. Akron.*
Maryland Historical Society photo.

Captain Kepner, Lt. Dugan and their mechanic, Sgt. Joseph Bishop, made a routine departure and soon found themselves bucking headwinds most of the way. The first part of the night was black as pitch. Still Dugan thrilled to look at the engine propellers on either side of the control car as they whirled efficiently, getting them all the time closer to their destination. He felt a real affection for motors. The props reflected the red running light on one side and green on the other. The vast expanse of Lake Erie was finally crossed and soon they were rising over mountains. The winds held them from their scheduled arrival by an extra three hours, but the landing at Lakehurst September 12 was without a hitch. Dugan sent another short wire to Frances: "Arrived today. Wonderful trip." The three tired aeronauts then got some sleep.

Dugan had been away from Frances Smith for a long time and now that he was qualified and had his own ship, they decided to get married, the date as yet unset.

Captain Kepner stayed for a five-day test in the hangar, designed to find out how much gas the ZMC-2 leaked every 24 hours. The men discovered that several bullet holes had been the cause of some leakage—people were always taking pot shots at blimps, particularly if the ship got too close to some rural still or hunters with an urge to shoot at something.

After Captain Kepner left, Lt. Dugan was skipper of the tin ship and began flying her on speed calibration and deceleration runs. He had reports to make as time progressed. One of his first flights in command took him and the ZMC-2 crew to New York, circling the Statue of Liberty, then along the Battery and up the North River over the steamer piers and below the tops of most of the buildings.

Landing at first was more difficult than in a conventionally designed blimp. After half-a-dozen flights, he felt he had made only one decent landing. This frustrated Dugan's search for perfection, and after making the last and worst landing he bawled out his rudderman. Later, he apologized.

With its stressed hull, the ZMC-2's effect of superheat was more noticeable. It was more difficult to rate when there was a sharp difference between the air temperature in the hull near the ground and that at normal operating altitude. In the rigid airship, superheat's effect was reduced somewhat by the airspace between the outer cover-ing and the gas cell within. The air circulation in the space presented a sudden temperature rise in the lifting gas, causing false lift.

On September 29, Jim Dugan had a futuristic type experience unlike anything he had ever known. Someone had to go inside the helium compartment of the new ZMC-2 and examine the wiring and the ballonets. He was the man. He put on a fabric helmet which had a glass window and two snouts for his air supply.

Looking like a creature from outer space (or more accurately inner space) he entered the compartment and the sleeve was tied off. The air was then sucked out with a vacuum cleaner and the suit's fabric pressed him tightly. All was black inside and he found it difficult to move his body. His mind was going a mile a minute—he felt like an unborn child. Then he wondered if he would suffocate if he wasn't getting enough air. He was on the verge of panic. Then he began using his flashlight. The wiring and the ballonets were in good shape. After he got out of the inspection suit, Dugan vowed to let others have the inspection duty if it came up again and they were of a persuasion to do so.

As the fall of 1929 continued, the ZMC-2 and the other blimps took many local flights. On October 10, Dugan had a delightful time greeting the big liners bound for Europe from New York. He would fly for seven hours, then be put on duty getting the Los Angeles into the hangar. On such occasions when gusty winds came up suddenly, he breathed an immense sigh of relief when the big ship was safely in the hangar.

Four days after the New York flight in the ZMC-2 and greeting the ocean liners, Dugan read with interest of the maiden voyage of the large new British rigid airship, R-101. That airship had been built by the government at its Cardington works. Another airship, the R-100, was not ready for flight. The R-100 was being constructed by private enterprise, under the leadership of Sir Dennistoun Burney of the Airship Guarantee Company at Howden. The specifications for both airships were identical, but it appeared from the start that the R-101 was destined to be a failure. The maiden voyage on October 14, 1929 revealed that it was dangerously overweight and underpowered. Ten flights were made and then to provide more lift the R-101 was lengthened by 46 feet.

On October 15, Lt. Jim Dugan submitted his

request for the Navy's post graduate course, encompassing a year at Annapolis and the second year at the Massachusetts Institute of Technology. Only a handful of candidates would be selected from all the naval aviators, both HTA and LTA. Dugan knew it would mean two years of the hardest work imaginable, but he felt it essential to furthering his career. He knew he could find some relaxation while at Annapolis if he made it, since he could get in his HTA flight time at the Naval Academy, where "yellow peril" seaplanes as well as multi-engine flying boats were based at North Severn for flight training. A week after asking for the PG course, Dugan signed on for another six years with the Navy, part of his obligation if the training were given him.

Frances Smith shared Dugan's keen interest in aviation, and in one of her letters early in November she wrote enthusiastically of the feat of the Dornier *DO-X,* which carried 169 people for an hour's flight. Dugan continued as a strong proponent of airships, asking her rhetorically where could one go in an hour? Having no reason to be disenchanted yet with the *R-101,* he pointed out that the new British government-built airship could carry 200 people and stay up thirty times as long at cruising speed. The *DO-X* with a hundred passengers could go 600 miles but the *R-101* could carry the same number 9,000 miles. He did admit that the airplane is uncomparably better for short hauls. The present airship was but a mere tugboat compared with the airships of two decades hence, he pointed out.

On November 6 Dugan lectured the station officers on the new metal ship. After his lecture, he was able to greet Commander Garland Fulton when he came in on the *Los Angeles* after a local flight. Fulton, right hand man to Admiral Moffett and "Mr. Airship" to the Bureau of Aeronautics chief, greeted Dugan warmly as he stepped down from the LA's control car. After exchanging pleasantries about the flight, Dugan asked a question:

"What are my chances for the postgraduate school, Commander?"

"Very good" answered Fulton. The Bureau had a strong say in which naval aviators would be picked; so Dugan felt that things were indeed going well with his application.

Dugan kept a vigorous schedule of flying the ZMC-2, since his mission was to continue flying the

Navy's unique new blimp until ordered elsewhere. On November 12, the designer of the *ZMC-2,* Ralph Upson, visited the station in his own airplane. After looking over his "child" and talking with Dugan about her handling qualities, he gave the airship pilot a ride in his plane.

Once airborne in Upson's monoplane, Dugan felt again the joy of getting his hands on the joy stick and feeling the rush of wind and the plane's response to his control. After the flight and Upson had departed, "Red" dashed off a letter to his fiancee. Before signing off he wrote that "airplanes have been your companions in my thoughts all afternoon. How I die to fly."

A week earlier, on November 7, at Akron, Ohio, Rear Admiral William A. Moffett drove a golden rivet into the first main ring of the first of two large airships to be constructed for the U.S. Navy. Rumor had it that the first ship, the *ZRS-4,* would probably be christened *U.S.S. Akron.* With luck, Lt. Dugan might serve aboard her someday.

A month later, Dugan heard that he would be going to PG school, but he was crushed to learn that instead of taking the course in airship structures he would be studying engines instead. An alternative was to study gas engineering, since the LTA people were interested in having people expert in the chemistry of various gaseous fuels and lifting gases. Dugan understood the pressures of the HTA people on the selection board to divide the students in courses which the board thought would be helpful to the Navy. Adding to the sting of what he considered defeat in not getting the course he wanted, Dugan heard from both Fulton and Rosendahl that his best bet might be to try and switch from studying engines to gas engineering, either one an anathema to Dugan.

Disconsolate, he walked up in the hangar to where he could look down on the top of the ZMC-2. He discovered the birds had scored about 100 per cent in hits on the ship. The resultant corrosion could be the cause of suspending operations, so he planned to have the ship cleaned thoroughly.

Dugan was down in the dumps. He turned away from the ZMC-2 and returned to his quarters thinking to himself "How are the mighty fallen!" He felt that one of his counselors had let him down in not helping him get the course he had banked upon. With mixed blessings, he read in the *Army-Navy Register* that he was indeed selected for PG in gas engineering. He set about immediately to appeal through channels to switch to a study of structures, backing it up with reasons why this would be more advantageous to the Service. Not many switches were made once the course selections had been printed, he knew.

On December 17, Col. Charles A. Lindbergh visited the station and again shook hands with his contemporary as well as with the other airship pilots at Lakehurst.

A week later, Cdr. Rosendahl congratulated Dugan on his selection for PG school and instructed him to break someone in on the *ZMC-2* and then come to "Rosie's" ship, the LA, for advanced rigid airship training before leaving for Annapolis in another five months.

Football-shaped Zeppelin metal clad No. 2 (*ZMC-2*), is powered by two 200 h. p. Wright Whirlwind engines, 149 feet 5 inches long. Cruising range: 600 miles.
Official U.S. Navy photo.

The U.S. Navy's only metalclad blimp *ZMC-2* was flown successfully for a dozen years. Her first skipper was Lt. (jg) Hammond James Dugan. Of 200,000 cubic foot capacity, the helium filled ship was a test vehicle to determine whether airships of larger size could have longer-lasting alclad covering vs. cotton.
(Copy of a Navy photo by the author).

CHAPTER THREE

Flying the Tin Ship

As January of 1930 ushered in cold, clear flying weather, Lt. (jg) Hammond James Dugan decided to try and dismiss from his mind his disappointment at not getting the course in aeronautical structures. He would fill in the five months before reporting to Postgraduate School bucking his frisky little *ZMC-2's* nose over most of the eastern section of the country. He had developed a special skill in flying the 200,000 cubic foot metalclad blimp, and he had faith in the reliability of the "bucking bronco's" twin 200 h.p. Wright Whirlwind engines. With her cruising radius of 600 miles, he expected to survey considerable countryside at a leisurely 62 miles an hour.

"Red's" daily routine at Lakehurst generally began with a look outside as soon as his eyes opened to see if it was raining or threatening. If the tops of the trees weren't swaying, Dugan felt his first taste of joy. There would be flying! The two training blimps would be taken from the hangar first, and then his crew would ready the metalclad, the last blimp in the enormous Hangar No. 1.

When weather was bad, Dugan would go to his desk in the flight office. A little later he would drive to the aerological office and have a look at the weather instruments and maps. If it still looked bad for flying, he would return to the office to work on the ship's log and reports of the metalclad's performance until 11:30 a.m. or noon. Lunch hour would be spent at the Bachelor Officers' Quarters, and then back to the office at one.

The afternoon would involve either more paper work or inspection of the ZMC-2. Because of the rapid transmission of heat to and from the helium, he could sometimes hear metallic "cries" of the hull in response to temperature changes. This didn't bother Dugan—it was inherent in the ship's design. At 4:10 p.m., he would return to the BOQ and play a brisk game of handball until 10 or 10:30 at night. Those days when he was weathered in were no joy. Flying had become his life.

Mid-winter flying was different than in summer as to comfort, even though skies were free of haze. January 16 he flew the tin ship for four hours with the thermometer between ten and fifteen degrees above zero. Dugan also saw duty on the *Los Angeles*, which when the weather was good stayed up for 32 hours at a time. Two or three flights a week made time pass swiftly.

January 20 was another bitter cold day, and Dugan arose at 6 a.m. and put on two suits of underclothes, two pairs of wool socks, two shirts, a muffler and a leather jacket. His first task was to work with the party getting the LA out and off. His breakfast, due to the airship's zero hour, was half an egg and part of a piece of toast.

Starting the engines of his *ZMC-2* took three-quarters of an hour. Hershey bars and a thermos of coffee helped alleviate the sharp bite of the cold. For flight, Dugan added a sweat shirt and a life preserver over his camel's hair-lined coveralls. Dugan's leather coat, gloves and helmet made moving about in his fleece-lined moccasins somewhat like a bear dancing in an ice box.

Despite the hard-to-start engines, the *ZMC-2* was airborne at 9:30 a.m. and not long afterward was crossing the Delaware River below Wilmington. Following the canal at low level, the metalclad crossed the Chesapeake Bay and headed on to Havre de Grace. Turning southward and following the railroad tracks, Dugan spied the Congressional Limited chugging along below at about 65 miles an hour. Dugan opened up the throttle and passed the train, which was 1,500 feet below the stubby blimp. Looking upward, the engineer ordered more coal shoveled on. Soon both train and blimp were making 75 miles an hour overground. Dugan came down to treetop level and dodged the trees as he waved to the passengers. Then he put the ship into a steep climb and in fifteen seconds the *ZMC-2* was back at a thousand feet above the ground.

Reaching Baltimore a few minutes after noon, the *ZMC-2* headed for the center of the city. Soon Dugan was weaving her skillfully about the Belvedere Hotel, nearby church spires and other tall buildings. He circled the neighborhood three times and on the fourth dropped a small package with a streamer on it that landed within ten feet of his mother's downtown home at 1015 Cathedral Street. A passing dentist, Dr. Joseph Fusco, picked up the shot-loaded rubberoid case and delivered it to the addressee. The elderly Mrs. Dugan waved a white cloth from the upper window of the three-story townhouse, but Dugan did not see her. He headed back for Lakehurst.

The next day's "Morning Sun" carried photos of Dugan's message and his mother's home. The coloring of the story made it into quite a stunt, and Dugan's message did nothing to help the situation. He wrote: "Hello, Mother: How do you like my new machine? Hammond."

Dugan had no idea his message would be read by nearly every adult Baltimorean. The newspaper reported that the "Tin bubble airship (was) down from Lakehurst to show it to (Dugan's) mother." He had staged the only front door, direct, air mail delivery on record, as hundreds watched. Dugan and his *ZMC-2* were at 4,000 feet, a brisk tailwind speeding his journey eastward to Lakehurst.

Near the Pennsylvania state line Dugan lost his way momentarily, but found it soon after crossing it. By 3:30 p.m. that Tuesday they were back at the station, and Dugan was happy to find two letters in his mailbox. The *Los Angeles* came back before he got a chance to read them, and he had to work with the party bringing her in.

After the LA was docked, Dugan was shown the Baltimore *Morning Sun* with its tongue-in-cheek report of his showing his mother his new "toy." He had been called for low flying twice before—the rules specified no flight below a thousand feet over the highest object on the ground. Dugan knew he was at 600 feet. The most damaging evidence was that the message came so close to its mark.

Well, he was 27 and next month he would be a ripe old 28. If you couldn't have a little fun now and then with their old ships he would as soon be on a destroyer plowing through the night at full power.

Friday he was called before the executive officer of the station. Surprisingly, nothing was said about Dugan's special message drop to his mother. Instead the exec talked about Dugan's assignment to write an instructive pamphlet on the ship as a guide to other pilots. It seemed as if the LTA family appreciated the publicity. No mention was made of his race with the Congressional Limited.

However, Station Order No. 3-30 came out shortly after his meeting with the executive officer. The subject: Aircraft Operations. "The attention of all pilots is called to Article 1332, BuAer Manual, which is quoted below: (5) Messages of an unofficial nature will not be dropped from non-rigid airships or airplanes attached to this station unless specifically authorized by the Commanding Officer." The order was signed by Cdr. Maurice R. Pierce, the station commanding officer.

As January ended Dugan watched with interest as the first glider was released from a dirigible at Lakehurst. The big new airship under construction at the Goodyear plant in Akron would carry five scouting aircraft in her belly. The initial experiments on the *Los Angeles* were developing the hook-on trapeze and working out other problems in such a revolutionary system for airships.

Dugan kept up his technical studying, but continued to relax with good literature. He was elated when the American writer Sinclair Lewis won the Nobel Prize in 1930.

In early February the *ZMC-2* was laid up while a new fuel system was installed, and Lt. Dugan gave instruction in one of the J-class blimps. His marriage was four months away, but as he flew the blimp above the cloud strata on February 5, the blue of the sky reminded him of his fiancee's eyes. The sun made the blimp's shadow on the clouds ghost-like as it slid snake-like over the crests and troughs. His carefree daydreaming stopped short when he realized that upon return to the station there would be a zero hour for the *Los Angeles* at midnight. Being an airshipman was certainly not a nine-to-five proposition, but he loved it.

Despite the usual winds of March, there were days when the weather was conducive to flying. In the middle of the month there was a calm in the winds and Dugan flew in the little ship until 11 at night.

On March 26 he learned that it was firm that he would be taking the aeronautical engineering course at M.I.T., once the year at Annapolis PG school was completed. Still unresolved was his assignment to take the engine specialist's course instead of a structures specialist course, the latter being more logical for airship work. The only real benefit he could see in knowing more about engines would be to fix up his Model A Ford, what with the crunch of the Depression. Dugan hoped that his requests through channels could somehow change the course he was now committed to, and he hoped that Commander Garland Fulton and Charles P. Burgess at BuAer could persuade the powers that be to change his assignment before he was committed to M.I.T. for the second year.

April came and between the showers Dugan began to increase his flying schedule. Frannie Smith occasionally read of the crashes that were a regular part of flying and questioned whether Dugan should consider going back to the relatively safer sea duty. He wrote her that he considered flying the safest mode of transportation. Besides, he added to his letter to her of April 2, 1930, he wasn't the type who gets killed. He also had to pass on the bad news that the Bureau of Navigation decided that neither fliers nor divers needed their additional duty compensation when going through two years of the post graduate school. For the soon-to-be wed Dugan, this meant a cut of $90 a month or a loss of $2,160 as a cost of becoming an aeronautical engineer!

April 12, 1930 started in the wee hours for Lt. Dugan and 400 other station personnel. He was up at 4 a.m. to land the *Los Angeles* and then he was out after breakfast to fly the *ZMC-2* in formation with the little ships up the Hudson.

Five days later he took his *ZMC-2* crew free ballooning. The balloon left at 3 p.m. and they had a delightful ride over northern New Jersey until at midnight, when it started raining. Dugan set her down on a farm near Cocheston Center, then with his soggy crew asked the farmer for a place to sleep in his barn. The farmer, who had never before had visitors drop in from the sky, provided them with hot coffee and showed them beds. The two crewmen of the *ZMC-2* and Dugan were thankful they

were the only ones along, since three beds were all that were available.

On April 25 he flew the tin ship for nine hours during the day and he was dead tired. Time was going swiftly, with the month that seemed so far away now almost over. He had received word that he was to take the *ZMC-2* down to Langley Field and operate from there while the *Graf Zeppelin* had a sojourn at Lakehurst and took up the space in the big hangar alongside the *Los Angeles.*

Frances wrote her fiancee of the color of that year's Kentucky Derby at Churchill Downs, wishing he could be there. Jockey Earl Sande won on "Gallant Fox," and then went on to take first in the Preakness in Baltimore.

By mid-May Dugan had broken in one of the other pilots on the tin ship, and he had a twinge of sadness to think that the day drew nigh when events would deprive him completely of his metal-clad charge. It was strange to be on the ground when his ship took off, watching the new man fly her. How funny it looked bouncing around like a little pig running backwards.

May 20th saw Captain Dugan of the tin ship engaged in the flying that thrilled him the most— going in formation with the other blimps up the Hudson River, a thousand feet above the Fleet off New York City. Ships were anchored from 60th Street to past 200th. Then the *ZMC-2* and her companions flew to Coney Island over the Narrows. The liner *Berengeria* was coming in from Europe and she blew her whistle, a pleasant deep-throated sound as the blimps dipped their bows in salute. They returned to Lakehurst after nine and a half hours of flying. Dugan was dismayed that radio announcer Floyd Gibbons wrongfully told the national audience of his news program that the *ZMC-2* had flown *under* one of the score of bridges surrounding Manhattan.

After that pleasant but long flight, Dugan's eyes were fatigued. He rested them by staying away from the books. He felt that if he could make his right eye strong enough for just a few more years, he would be almost willing to give it away to be able to continue flying.

On Thursday, May 27 Dugan and the *ZMC-2* wended their way after a midnight departure just off the surface of the water down the coast to Langley Field, Virginia. He would stay until the *Graf* departed about May 31st, unless she needed repairs, which could add another week.

Dugan felt like a fish out of water at the Army Air Base. He wished he had brought his books with him—what a tremendous amount of studying he could have done. It was different than being at Lakehurst, where if one had to loaf, which was seldom, at least one did it among friends. Outside the dismal barracks, Dugan could hear the sound of plane motors. The engine "music" brought on the old urge for Heavier-Than-Air the more he heard it.

On May 30, 1930 the annual International Schneider Cup Seaplane Race was scheduled to be held at the Anacostia Naval Air Station, with the airship *Los Angeles* attending. Lt. Ralph Barnaby, the Navy's pioneer glider-soaring officer was slated to fly a glider from the airship's trapeze and land on the air station during the race program.

Several days before the event, however, Barnaby was stricken with the flu. Lt. "Tex" Settle, in charge of the Naval inspection team in connection with Goodyear-Zeppelin Corporation's construction of the new airship *ZRS-4* and an organizing member of the Akron Glider Club, volunteered to "pinch-hit" for Barnaby.

About midnight May 29 the *Los Angeles*, commanded by Cdr. Vince Clarke, departed Lakehurst with the Navy's German-built Prüfling training glider on her airplane trapeze. During the midwatch, rough air caused a small rip in the Prüfling's port wing fabric. By forenoon, continued rough air as the LA approached Washington caused the rip to expand.

Captain Clarke held the airship to minimum speeds to ease the loads on the glider, but the hole in the wing fabric kept growing slowly. The southwesterly wind at 2,000-3,000 feet was brisk.

By early afternoon the airship was leeward of Anacostia. There was no way to repair the wing in flight. Lt. Settle judged that, despite some loss of lift due to the hole in the wing, he could make it over the low escarpment at the leeward end of the landing field, with a little help from thermals and an up-draft that he counted on over the escarpment.

Settle climbed down the trapeze and into the glider. At about 2,200 feet altitude he released the Prufling. Soon he realized the thermals were disappointing. As he approached the escarpment only a hundred feet over the tree tops it looked as if he would not make it. Looking over the built-up part of the town of Anacostia, he searched for a place

on which to set the glider down. In an enclosing wall, he spotted a large building with a courtyard into which he might be able to slip the glider. Approaching, he saw several hundred people in the yard. They had cleared the court's center for his landing and were shouting and waving to him to come on.

Just before he drove into the courtyard, the missing up-draft arrived from over the escarpment. Settle got just the amount of needed lift to zoom over the tree tops with a few feet of clearance. The sudden gift of air helped him dive successfully onto the Naval Air Station landing field, as thousands of spectators applauded.

Emerging from the cockpit, Settle inquired:

"What was that large building with all the friendly people?"

Amid the crowd, voices answered:

"That's Saint Elizabeth's Mental Hospital!"

As the days dragged on at Langley for the Navy pilot among the Army airmen, Dugan made friends with the pursuit ship pilots. He had a natural enthusiasm for their HTA activity at Langley, and nothing was more fascinating to him than a speedy little pursuit plane humming over the field at 150 miles an hour. He was lonely at Langley, and his stay had been lengthened because the *Graf* had taken a side trip. His marriage was only two weeks away and married life would be Paradise compared to the lonely quarters *sans* desks for writing or reading at Langley.

Finally the eight-day sojourn of the *ZMC-2* was over and June 5 saw the tin ship heading back to Lakehurst via Baltimore. When Dugan reached Catonsville, he flew over "Bonnie Doone," his family home at Nunnery Lane. He had telephoned the clan that he might fly over, weather permitting, and the family was out to wave when the roar of the Wright Whirlwinds signified his presence overhead.

Upon landing at Lakehurst, he turned the ship over to his relief, then got a good night's sleep. The next day he went on 15 days leave, to return the 21st to be detached and then report to the Annapolis PG school June 30, 1930.

At the bachelor's dinner two days before the marriage, Dugan winced at the news that the German boxer, Max Schmeling, defeated the American Jack Sharkey for the world heavyweight championship. "Red" had not gotten over his anti-German feeling, since World War I ended just two years before his matriculation at the Naval Academy. Schmeling was only 24, three years younger than Sharkey, and his 188 pounds let him move faster than Sharkey's extra nine pounds. Dugan hoped Sharkey would have another go at the German in a year or two, and go a lot more than just four rounds.

A large wedding took place in Lexington, Kentucky June 14. The bride and groom, both 27, had courted for eight years. By not marrying earlier, he had time to qualify in the field of his choice. She in turn had graduated Phi Beta Kappa from the University of Kentucky, and had studied at the New York Public Library and at Simmons College, Boston. Since Dugan's lovely brunette was a member of the Junior League, the wedding received generous coverage in the newspapers.

One of his ushers, who came down from Lakehurst to Lexington for the wedding, told him that in June the *Los Angeles* had successfully outflown a storm which threatened to engulf her on her return from a local cruise. Faced with a strong storm approaching from the south, the LA was flown eastward out to sea and allowed the storm to pass between her and the coast. Then she was able to dock without incident at the station. Dugan breathed a sigh of relief that the ship was not lost and hence had not set the program back a decade.

The newlyweds arrived in Annapolis after a short honeymoon and Lt. (jg) Dugan reported to Postgraduate School. They rented an attractive white cottage in Ferry Farms, a community on the north banks of the Severn river within a bicycle ride of the school over the six-year old drawbridge. Dugan soon found himself immersed in the curriculum in the Spanish-type building, located near the baseball diamond and reached by the first gate (No. 8) of the academy when approaching from the north. For relaxation, they sailed the academy boats and played tennis on the many courts available to Navy families.

That summer the Dugans were thrilled by the trans-Atlantic flight of the privately-built airship *R-100*. With a crew of 44, including Squadron Leaders R. S. Booth and G. H. Scott, she flew from Britain to Canada and back. The end of July and middle of August the newspaper headlines were full of the achievement. While the "socialist" airship had succeeded, the government airship *R-101* still needed to prove her mettle.

The Dugans even had time for some golf while at Annapolis, although "Red" was better with the slip-stick which he had to practice with for his PG school courses than with his clubs, since there was little time for achieving perfection on the links. Still, it was relaxing to play with other Navy couples. On September 27, they read in the newspapers of Bobby Jones' latest win. The popular champ from Atlanta was the first in the sport to hold the four highest golf titles at one time.

On October 5 the proponents of LTA were distressed to hear that the airship *R-101*, whose weight of 230,720 pounds approximated that of the Navy's *ZRS-4* a-building, had crashed and burned in France, killing 48 men. Political expediency and the inherently heavy construction of the ship contributed to the disaster. Lord Thompson, a cabinet member, wished to fly to India for a meeting and be back for an Imperial conference in London October 20. He urged that the ship leave England October 4 to meet his schedule, with the implication that if the *R-101* did not meet his schedule, there wouldn't be further government-sponsored work on airships. Against the better judgment of the *R-101's* captain, Flight Lt. H. Carmichael Irwin, and without adequate tests for her airworthiness beforehand, the ship left on the fourth. She had never undergone a trial either in poor weather or at full speed. Her cells were leaky and when she reached Beauvais, France she flew into a hillside and her hydrogen exploded. Only a crisp carcass of twisted girders remained over the countryside the next morning.

Jim Dugan was distressed and so upset about the *R-101* that for days he and his bride talked about little else. "Red" had not lost confidence in airships, but he knew the disaster would halt the future for that mode of transportation for years in Britain.

"If only they had had helium," he told Frances "at least the fire would not have happened."

"Perhaps our country should not hoard helium so selfishly," she replied.

He had been puffing on his pipe while trying to study. With the arrival of each new account of the crash they poured over the new information and discussed the tragedy.

"No one will ever really know the true cause" Dugan explained to his wife. "The enlisted men who survived don't know enough about aviation to pinpoint the trouble."

"Even if she ran through a storm," Frances said,

"She should have gone through, as the *Graf Zeppelin* so often does."

As the days went on, the investigation reports helped Dugan understand why the *R-101* was doomed, contrary to the earlier reports which had made him confident of her possibilities. The manufacturers had substituted a heavy yet shallow ring of a small triangular cross section in the skeleton without the vitally needed internal transverse bracing essential to good construction. The disregard of the fundamental need for strength was a cause of the wreck, together with a low buoyancy factor where useful load was only 27 per cent of her gross lift. She had then been given a modification to give another half-million cubic feet, but useful load was still only 36 percent of gross lift. With leaky cells, poor lift and poor internal bracing, she was a natural not to survive the first unstable weather. "Get-there-itis" was never conducive to aviation safety, particularly without a thorough pre-testing of the airship.

Girder construction for the two lower keel walkways are seen in the protuberant girders in the lower part of the giant ring as it is hauled into place in the Goodyear Zeppelin airdock.
Goodyear Tire and Rubber Company photo.

CHAPTER FOUR

Birth of the Airship Akron

During the 1930-31 period when Lt. (jg) Hammond James Dugan and his bride Frances were living on the north bank of the Severn River and he was completing his first year of the Postgraduate School, Lt. "Tex" Settle, his former ballooning instructor, was assigned to duty at the Goodyear-Zeppelin Company at Akron, Ohio. Settle headed the Navy inspectors concerned with the building of the new *ZRS-4* rigid which when completed would probably be christened the *U.S.S. Akron.* At least, the Navy Department had received enough requests to that effect from civic organizations, veterans groups and business officials to make it almost a foregone conclusion.

A frequent contact of Lt. Settle's was Cdr. Garland Fulton, who came to Akron regularly to keep abreast of the progress of this first of two scouting airships. Fulton, second man in his class at the Naval Academy, had long been Rear Admiral William Moffett's right hand man on lighter-than-air matters. The two men—Settle, dark complected and with a short haircut, and the round-faced Fulton, hair parted in the middle—frequently toured the big shed in which the construction proceeded. It had orange peel doors to reduce the problem of gusty crosswinds and was so tall that clouds sometimes formed at the top. Rain showers were not completely unknown inside.

The shed was open to the public, but only to about 20 feet inside the doors. There people could stand in awe at the enormous ship, which would be 785 feet long when built and stand 15 stories high. Workmen at the top of the hangar and on ladders looked like midgets from where the people stood. When they tired of watching the workers assembling the duralumin framework and guying with piano-like steel wiring, the spectators inspected the railroad spur track outside with its tank cars bearing helium containers from the Fort Worth helium fields.

The design history of the *ZRS-4* started six years earlier in 1924. The Navy had two airships, the *Shenandoah* built in this country and the *Los Angeles* constructed in Germany. The Bureau of Aeronautics started a Design No. 60 to keep abreast of the art. The new airship would have about six million cubic feet gas volume, so that it could fit into the big hangar at Lakehurst and could fly the Atlantic round trip without refueling. The design was carried along until 1927, when authorization came for two new airships and a design competition was announced. The next year, a second competition was announced. Goodyear-Zeppelin Corporation submitted three designs. Schuette—Lanz of Germany made a design, as did the American Brown Boveri Electric Corporation. All were good and received a rating of eighty or higher, with Goodyear-Zeppelin the winner.

Somewhat fatter than the *Los Angeles,* with a length/diameter ratio of 5.91 to 1.00, the larger *ZRS-4* or *U.S.S. Akron,* in essence resembled the LA in appearance. The new ship would have 77 men and a dozen officers, plus a half-dozen pilots for the hook-on planes yet to be constructed making out the crew complement. Normal flying crew would be 38 men and 10 officers plus pilots.

The *Akron* design differed to the layman in its rather sizeable empennage, auxiliary vanes for balancing on the rudders; a rather small, protruding control car; internal engine rooms; eight 560-horsepower engines and propellers driven through gearing which could be tilted to give thrust in four directions. An internal hangar aft of the control car would house five airplanes. Resilient bulkheads

Not unlike a giant watermelon form made of duralumin, the *ZRS-4* is well underway December 2, 1930 at the Goodyear Zeppelin airdock. Note bow portion in lower right.
J. Christian Fenger photo.

Below: A construction ring of the *Akron*, ready to be hauled into place in the airdock at Goodyear Zeppelin Corporation, Akron, Ohio.
Goodyear Tire & Rubber Co. photo.

provided a check for surging gas cells in the event one deflated. A strong point was made in the lower fin for use in mooring and handling. Two corridors along the lower sides of the ship and one at the top centerline was a new development, to expedite getting easier and better access to all parts of the hull.

The ship would be comprised of 36 longitudinal girders. Twelve enormous gas cells would be placed between main frames, spaced 74 feet apart. Acres of cotton would cover the skeleton, with a life expectancy of seven years. Each fabricated piece of 17SRT duralumin was anodically treated to ward off corrosion. Before the last drawing of wires, galvanizing was performed. Other steel parts underwent cadmium- or zinc plating.

Engines were the Maybach, Model VL-11, developed from the 420 horsepower engines of the *Los Angeles*. The *Akron's* engines would have 560 horsepower at 1,600 r.p.m. Each engine, of 12-cylinder, 60-degree V-design, weighed dry about 2,600 pounds. Each engine room had a floor space of about eight square feet, and engines were reached from side corridors through doors. Placed athwartships, each engine drove a 16-foot transverse shaft to its short, tiltable propeller shaft. Transmission gearing reduced the 1,600 r.p.m. to 925 r.p.m. for the propellers, a speed reduction of .578. Each two-bladed wooden prop was 16 feet four inches in diameter. Prop rotation would be staggered and would turn opposite to the one ahead or astern.

Water recovery to balance off the loss in weight as fuel was burned off was done through five panels mounted close to the hull above each of the eight engines. The panels consisted of aluminum tubes connected by headers. In theory, 135 pounds of water could be recovered for every 100 pounds of aviation gasoline burned.

The giant airship would carry 126,000 pounds of gasoline stored in 110 tanks. Extensive piping allowed the transfer of fuel along the length of the ship. Twenty-eight water ballast storage bags were provided in the design, each of 400 pounds capacity, with four bags of half that capacity. Ballast was dropped by wire pulls from the control car.

The 65-pound strength cotton was sewed into panels 74 feet long by either a foot or two-feet wide, which were laced through eyelets into position with ramie cord and were secured to the hull framework. Once laced into the framework, the cover received four coats of acetate dope, the last two containing aluminum powder. Nearly 33,000 square yards were required to cover the ship.

Because of the enormous size of the *Akron's* twelve gas cells, the weight of the upper quarter of the cells was increased to 3-ounce cotton cloth, coated with rubber and given a final coating of paraffin. Another fabric, of a combination gelatin-latex was used on the even-numbered cells and the off-numbered cells were of the rubber fabric just developed. A total of 54,000 square yards (21+ acres) were required for the cells, weighing some 22,000 pounds which under high humidity would increase by an additional five per cent. Valves for releasing helium were located along the upper corridor and were uniformly 32-inches in diameter.

To facilitate equalizing air pressure in the hull with the outside air pressure, openings were provided along the side corridors so that interior pressure in the outer cover would equalize quickly when the airship rose or rapidly descended suddenly.

To guard against surging of cells in the event that the airship would pitch in rough air, bulkheads were designed to be resilient. In the stiff main frames, these bulkheads were installed, looking not unlike a spider's web. If a cell deflated, its neighbors could not surge into the space.

Electrical power was needed for radio, lighting, telephones and partly for cooking, as well as for pumps, winches and fans. Two eight kilowatt, 110-volt D.C. generators driven by an internal combustion engine comprised the power source. The electrical installation was similar to that of a small surface vessel's needs, and existing commercial apparatus was used. In future airships, Cdr. Garland Fulton and the designers at the Bureau of Aeronautics as well as at Goodyear-Zeppelin hoped manufacturers would develop weight saving equipment for lighter-than-air ship usage.

Westinghouse designed a weight and space saving radio outfit for the *Akron* with which Cdr. Fulton was quite pleased, and in inspection trips to visit Lt. "Tex" Settle, he showed approval of the communications setup. Settle, formerly communications officer of the *U.S.S. Shenandoah* and also the *U.S.S. Los Angeles*, was equally pleased. The *Akron* had an intermediate frequency transmitter (300-605 kilocycles) and a high frequency transmitter (3,000-18,100 kilocycles), with a range of 5,000 nautical miles on high frequency and 500

Construction progress on the *ZRS-4* is seen in this picture taken at the Goodyear
Zeppelin airdock on March 1, 1931.

J. Christian Fenger photo

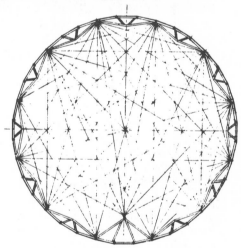

SECTION AT STA 198.75

nautical miles for the former. Facsimile equipment to receive weather maps and similar data were hoped for in the future. A hundred-foot antenna was installed along the hull and 800 feet of wire could be dropped from the outboard side of the radio room.

The telephone system consisted of a 20 to 30-volt manually operated switchboard located in the control car.

Eighteen telephones were located through the ship. Three conversations could take place at any one time, or an alarm could be sounded on all telephones. Voice tubes also were provided between the control room and nearby spaces. As in previous airships, mechanical engine telegraphs operated from the control room to engine rooms.

The control room, unlike the suspended car of the *Shenandoah,* or the rather large car of the *Los Angeles,* was streamlined and compact. The forward third contained rudder and elevator controls, gas and ballast controls, engine telegraphs, and instruments needed for flying. The middle third was a navigating compartment, and the after third an access point for the ladder into the hull. As in the earlier *Shenandoah,* an emergency control station was located in the stern, in the *Akron's* case at the bottom of the lower fin. Both the control room forward and the emergency control point had rattan bumpers. Above the control car forward were the radio and aerological rooms, plus an office space and a photo laboratory.

Rudder and elevator controls required ten turns of the rudder or elevator wheels from hard over to hard over. Because the control cables ran three city-blocks in length, equalizing devices were employed to remove the slack. De-clutching would throw either one of the pair of rudders or pair of elevators out of action, and steering could be shifted from the control room forward to the after emergency control station.

Along either side of the *Akron's* airplane compartment were the living accommodations. For structural reasons the Bay VII area was divided into eight spaces, each with an 8 by 10 foot floor area. The crew's toilet and wash room were on the port side. Seven similar spaces were each fitted with four canvas bottom bunks and lockers. On the starboard side from aft forward were the generator room, galley, crew's mess, CPO mess, officers' mess and two rooms each with four bunks for the officers. Other rooms were located further forward above the control room.

To view the scenery below, one had to go into a corridor and look through an inclined cellon-covered window. Living spaces received heat through aluminum piping running from the forward engine rooms.

The airplane compartment with T-shaped hatch was 70 feet long by 32 feet wide. Five Curtiss *F9C2* airplanes, at a construction cost of about $22,965 apiece, specially sized to fit the opening, were designed for the airship.

Parts of the structure were as high as a fifteen-story building. Correct alignment of the lace-like structure was achieved using overhead cranes, movable platforms, extension ladders and other equipment to help reach any part of the airship.

The polygonal frames were assembled horizontally on the floor and then positioned in the vertical, followed by placement of the longitudinals and shear- and netting wires. The amidships bay was erected first, progressing forward and then shifted to working towards the stern. Hundreds of tests were made on girders, joints, fittings, fins, rudders, elevators and the various items of installation and equipment.

The airship was expected to be about five per cent over the designed weight estimate.

Time schedules were met in most instances.

March 1930 had seen the first main frame assembled on the floor. Eight months later, seven bays were erected. By January of 1931, the hull structure was practically complete, except for fins, rudders and elevators. By April, the outer cover was partially in place, and the part near the bow had received a final coat of aluminized dope. July of 1931 saw power plants installed, with drive gear, propellers, radiators and water recovery apparatus installed. Control surfaces, as big inside as a family living room, were being positioned. Maximum air speed called for in the specifications was 72.5 knots under standard trial conditions.

A modification had been made in the original design. Originally, the fins were long and slender, running 110 feet. They were to be attached to main frames 0, 17.5 and 35. The Bureau of Aeronautics decided that, because this prevented a view of the lower fin, the fins would be shorter and deeper. The fin leading edges would have been anchored to frame 35. Leading edges, in the change, were now anchored to intermediate frame 28.75, in a flimsier manner. The attachments at frame 17.5 were loaded higher as a result. Increasing the depth of the fins therefore increased

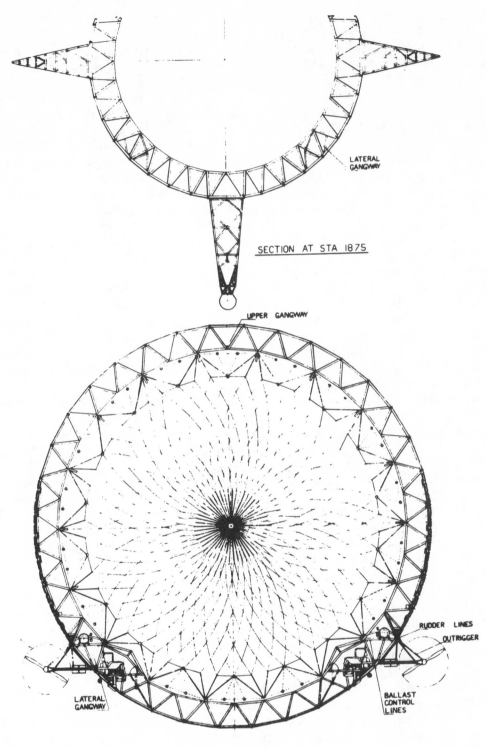

SECTION AT STA. 1875

LATERAL GANGWAY

UPPER GANGWAY

RUDDER LINES

OUTRIGGER

BALLAST CONTROL LINES

LATERAL GANGWAY

SECTION AT STA. 102.5

AKRON

the leverage of lateral loads. Those who decreed the change felt that moving the control car eight feet toward the stern and shortening the fins gave the operational benefit desired. They felt that the attachment of the leading edges of the fins was no hazard to flight safety, since the fins could withstand side gusts up to 34 m.p.h. A limiting condition in the *Akron* design was the "gust condition." The airship was assumed to fly at full power perpendicularly into a sharply defined gust— moving at 50 feet per second. This was 60 per cent greater than the criteria for transport airplanes. The expectation was that the ship could stand twice that, or gusts up to 68 miles an hour.

By the spring of 1931, Lt. (jg) Jim Dugan at Annapolis PG School and the rest of the Navy aviators in lighter-than-air were excited that the *Akron* would be ready in June. Officers in LTA were tense to see who would be chosen for her crew.

On May 12-14, 1931, "Red" Dugan attended and presented a paper at the 5th National Academy of Sciences meeting in his hometown of Baltimore for the American Society of Mechanical Engineers. It was near the end of the first half of his postgraduate schooling. He also found time from his studies to visit Commander Charles Rosendahl in Washington. Uppermost in his mind was the switching of his course at M.I.T. from engines to airship structures.

Meanwhile, the PG course continued. On June 29, 1931, Dugan had an enjoyable three-hour "bull session" with math professors at the Naval Academy. They got on the subject of rocket trips to the moon and came up with the opinion that it was a distinct possibility for the future.

In mid-July, Dugan got word that he and a fellow officer named Combs were to register for the course in engineering, the bugaboo that he had lived with all year. Dugan was dejected. He fired off a letter to Commander Garland Fulton asking for advice.

In discussing the matter with Combs, Dugan seemed resigned to his fate, but he wasn't going to give up without a struggle.

"If it turns out that they want an engine specialist," Dugan said, "that's all there is to it."

Combs, who was his contemporary but was more interested in the engine course, agreed. "It's a dirty trick, since you were the one who got the PG School ball rolling from Lakehurst, Red."

"I fought so hard for the structures course the year before last," Dugan said. "Maybe I should look at the brighter side—look at the repair bills Franny and I will save on our Ford."

Frances Dugan was away for a few weeks visiting her relatives. When he wrote her about the situation, she wrote him a strong letter saying that perhaps he was being puerile about the Navy's assignment of the course. Her letter brought him up short—he told her in reply that "the sailor's wife surpassed the sailor in his own field. The very thoughts clouded the atmosphere with such a blue haze that I sometimes could not see the paper before me."

Dugan had expressed a threat to leave the service and seek employment in private industry in aviation. He nevertheless had promised not to resign before three years from the completion of the course, and signed papers to that effect.

When Frances returned, his "ship" was back on course. After his studies, they relaxed on the porch of their rented house on the north bank of the Severn, across the river from where the white Spanish ship *Reina Mercedes* was moored. The young couple had many discussions about war. Frances was a pacifist.

"Military men are probably the least eager for war," Dugan said. "After all, they are the ones who are killed first. But I don't believe the world is ready for disarmament, Franny."

They would also discuss the decreased allowances in the budget for military preparedness. The depression was in full swing.

Dugan received a cordial reply from his friend, Cdr. Garland Fulton, in the Bureau of Aeronautics. Fulton advised him to put in a request at once for the general course in airship structures, giving all his reasons for desiring it. Trying every avenue he could think of, Dugan also wrote Captain H. E. Shoemaker, whom he felt had never had any love for the Heavier-Than-Air people in the Bureau and their attitude toward LTA. He pointed out that M.I.T. had two LTA courses, one in airship theory and the other in structures, neither of which he was scheduled to take, despite his Lakehurst training.

He fumed that the "fools in Annapolis and in the Bureau ought to start discovering they are alive."

Finally on July 20, 1931 he received news that made him ecstatic. He had obtained the structures

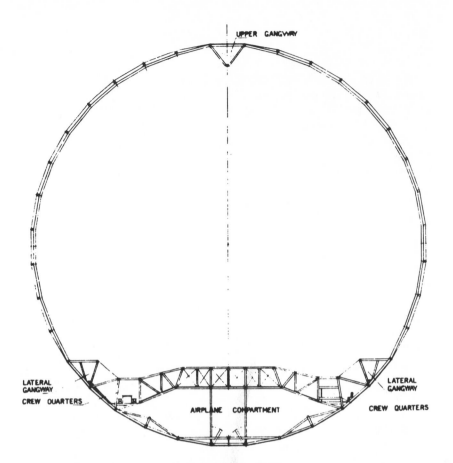

UPPER GANGWAY

LATERAL GANGWAY

CREW QUARTERS

AIRPLANE COMPARTMENT

LATERAL GANGWAY

CREW QUARTERS

SECTION AT STA 131.25

The *U.S.S. Akron* moored to the "Iron Horse" at Lakehurst.
Official U.S. Navy photo.

course instead of engines. He had done so much studying that a week later he noticed his eyes were bothering him again. His left eye was still doing all the work, and he planned to see a doctor to see why his right eye suffered from lack of exercise.

The official letter authorizing the switch in courses came a month later, and the Dugans were already moved into a great ark of a house in Belmont, Mass. from which he could commute to M.I.T. The letter was from the Chief, BuAer to the Head of the PG School through the Naval Academy Superintendent, and was dated August 28, 1931. The letter explained that the Bureau's original intention to have one LTA man and one HTA man take the engine specialist course was based on general considerations and the idea was to equalize the number of students taking the various courses. While the Bureau granted that an engine specialist course would be of greater value to a student in Heavier-Than-Air, the Bureau now considered a structures specialist course would be a better foundation for airship work. BuAer therefore modified its previous recommendation and now would be glad to see both students given a structures course, including a reasonable amount of study about engines.

The Dugans were on leave while awaiting the start of the M.I.T. course, ensconsed in the big mansion of a long-time friend, Charles Morton. Drawn together by their mutual interest in literature, the Dugans were at once at home with Morton, a talented editor who wrote for the top Boston newspaper and contributed frequently to national magazines, such as *The New Yorker* and *Atlantic Monthly*. He had had offers to head the staff of the latter magazine, and it was likely that he would accept in the near future.

The short vacation had its moments of activity as well as philosophical reflection. Frances enjoyed the quiet moments with Hammond—she preferred that name for her husband over the Jim or "Red" which so many of his Academy friends used. Carrying their first child, she watched with pleasure as Dugan lay on his back in the grass at the Morton estate, studying summer cloud formations and birds soaring in the sky. Or he would bend over a brook, run his hand through the water and watch the effect of varying speed on the interflow and turbulence of the water. She knew that in his mind he was translating what he observed into similar movement of air currents for the time when he would again be flying on one of the big airships.

These moments of solitude were varied with frequent HTA flights in a helldiver piloted by Navy pilot, LCdr. John King. One August afternoon they took a flight up the coast to Cape Ann, flying low over the water with the wing tip figuratively brushing the rocks along the shoreline. Investigating various islands, they exulted in the freedom of flight, zooming over lighthouses until they reached Rockport. Then they landed on a hard beach on the other side of the Cape.

While they walked on the beach, Dugan asked King to do some stunts on the return flight. He obliged and Dugan realized he still loved HTA flight, despite his commitment to LTA. After the final loop and spin, they noticed thunderstorms were developing and they made a dash for the airport. The raindrops in the open-cockpit ship felt like needles on their faces. They landed in a downpour, wet but happy. When they arrived back at the Morton house, they downed a highball "for medicinal purposes."

The M.I.T. course commenced, and Dugan was off each morning after breakfast. He had elected to have a wooden model of the *Akron* made to scale, 30 inches long. For his thesis, he would have the model "flown" in the wind tunnel and draw conclusions on ground handling of a big rigid and the effect of gusts. Along the sides of the model, from stem to stern, tiny copper pipes ran, only 1/32 of an inch in diameter and set apart by 3/4 of an inch. The pipes lay in grooves in the wood, flush with the surface. At half-inch intervals the length of the pipes, holes were drilled which could be stopped. By stopping some holes and leaving others open, Dugan would be able to find the wind pressure on any given portion of the airship.

One night in September, after Dugan's hour's nap following dinner before he went to work on math calculations until one, two and sometimes three in the morning as had become his habit, the grind was interrupted by a visit from an old friend. It was the airship *Los Angeles,* her lights twinkling and the moon shining on her silver hull over the Morton house. "Red" had just taken a shower, and Frances had been napping. They were so excited that they rushed out of the house with almost nothing on—they didn't want to miss getting a good look at the ship. He looked forward to the day when the course would be completed and he might be with the crew of the *U.S.S. Akron,* which

The *Akron* outside the Goodyear
Zepplin airdock just before her
first flight September 23, 1931.
J. Christian Fenger photo.

Below: Invitation, same source.

Goodyear - Zeppelin Corporation

requests the honor of your presence

at the christening of the

United States Airship Akron

Mrs. Herbert Hoover, Sponsor

Saturday afternoon, the eighth of August

One thousand nine hundred and thirty-one

at two-thirty o'clock

Akron, Ohio

on September 23rd had its initial flight out in Ohio.

In November, in a brief respite from his studies, Dugan took another exciting flight with John King in the helldiver. They zoomed over the house. Frances, whose confinement had been relieved by the delivery of their infant boy, watched as the plane did rolls, dives, turns and spins. Limp and quivery with excitement, she grabbed diapers and sheets off the line and waved to the aerobats over-head. "Red" stood up in the front cockpit and waved. Then they climbed to 18,000 feet and she could see them no longer. Dugan found it hard to breathe in the rarified air, but he exulted in a spectacular view of Massachusetts and six other states.

The year of 1931, drawing to a close as Dugan was closeted with his M.I.T. studies, saw Heavier-Than-Air making the headlines. In January, the first formation flight across the South Atlantic, from Portuguese Guinea to Natal, Brazil was made by ten seaplanes under the command of General Italo Balbo. Six months later, Wiley Post and Harold Gatty flew around the world in the Lock-heed *Winnie Mae.* They completed 15,474 miles in eight days, 15 hours and 51 minutes. October 3-5, 1931, Clyde Pangborn and Hugh Herndon made the first non-stop flight from Japan to the United States, landing their Bellanca at Wenatchee, Washington.

Dugan felt these achievements boded well for airplanes, but he still felt the superiority of the airship for long flights without needing to land for refueling.

Other news gave him pause to think of the need for greater preparedness. The explosion on the Manchurian railway in mid-September had given Japan a pretext to begin occupation of Manchuria. He felt that the scouting capabilities of the *Akron* and later her sister ship, the *ZRS-5,* might prove valuable in scouting the Pacific Ocean frontier in the future as the Land of the Rising Sun's fleet spread farther afield.

One of the *Akron's* eight swivelling external propellers, with part of the water recovery units above. Taken August 20, 1931.
Goodyear Tire & Rubber Co. photo.

White smoke from steam engines behind Washington's Union Station dot railroad tracks as the *Akron*
flies over the Main Post Office and the Government Printing Office of the nation's capital.
Below, overflying an industrial section of another city at cruising altitude.
Official U.S. Navy photos.

CHAPTER FIVE

Rosendahl in Command

Following the early trial flights of the *Akron,* the Navy commissioned the airship at 8 p.m. Tuesday, Oct. 27, 1931. She was formally attached to the Rigid Airship Training and Experimental Squadron at Lakehurst, with LCdr. Charles E. Rosendahl her captain.

Six years had passed since the tall and then lean "Rosie" had been catapulted to fame as the senior surviving officer aboard the ill-fated *U.S.S. Shenandoah.* Since that time he had several years in command of the *Los Angeles,* which after the loss of the former airship was flown more cautiously. He had put on some weight in the intervening years, and in his leather flight jacket he made an impressive looking skipper indeed. Besides his Navy flying experience, he had made the round-the-world flight on the *Graf Zeppelin,* and was one of the top spokesman for the case for the airship in presentations before the Congress and to Navy higher-ups.

The airship personnel were a small family in comparison with other elements of the service. With the crew that were mustered for the commissioning were seven enlisted men who had flown on the *Shenandosh:* Charles Solar, ACMM; Joe Shevlowitz, AMM1C; Bill Russell, ACMM; August Quernheim, ACMM; Ralph Jones, ACMM; Dick Deal, BM2C; and Art Carlson, CBM. "Shev" had been in the torn-off bow section of the *Shenandoah* when "Rosie" and a handful of others free-ballooned and landed the bow on the Nichols farm near Sharon, Ohio. Rosendahl as senior officer had received the Distinguished Flying Cross. Dick "Lucky" Deal had missed that final flight. For a year now he had been married to the widow of Ralph Joffray, one of the 14 men lost in the wreck of the *Shenandoah* Sept. 3, 1925.

As they mustered in the big hangar at Lakehurst, the commissioning was broadcast over the NBC network over station WEAF. Announcer Graham McNamee introduced John Philip Sousa, who conducted the band in a spirited arrangement of "Anchors Aweigh" from New York City. Then McNamee introduced Rosendahl, whose words were followed by a message from President Litchfield of the Goodyear-Zeppelin Corporation. From Baltimore, aboard the "Constitution," Secretary of the Navy Charles Francis Adams gave his remarks, followed by David Ingalls, Assistant Secretary of the Navy (Air) Rear Admiral William Moffett followed from Washington. Finally, Captain H. E. Shoemaker read orders from the Chief of Naval Operations accepting the ship, "Rosie" then read his orders to command and ordered the watch set and the crew piped down.

With the brand new ship, considerable local flights were in store to shake her down. The Saturday after her commissioning, the filling of gas cells to 100 per cent fullness was completed, then lowered to 88 per cent full of helium. In readying the *Akron* for the next flight, 650 pounds of spare engine parts and 500 pounds of food were placed on board. Monday the second day of November the signal for general assembly was sounded at 4:30 in the morning. Gas cells were now 87 per cent full. Ten officers, 49 men, 31 representatives of the press and 19 guests made a total of 109 persons aboard.

From the control car, Rosendahl ordered engines 3, 4, 7 and 8 tilted to help with lift off.

"All engines ahead, two thirds speed," was his next command. The engine telegraphs relayed the signal to the engine cars.

At 7:10 a.m. they were in the air, with all

A crewman stands at the rudder wheel of the
Akron in the Goodyear Zeppelin Corporation
drydock September 18, 1931. Note the flashlight
in his back pocket, necessary for inspecting
the airship's interior. Seats are used by the
officer conning the rudderman.
J. Christian Fenger photo.

engines standard speed.

"Course 270 degrees," the captain ordered.

The navigator made quick calculations for a ten
degree west variation and 19 degrees wind drift,
making the track 241 degrees.

By 9:21 a.m. the *Akron* was over Maryland's
capital, Annapolis, and the midshipmen of the
academy saw their first glimpse of the silver-hued
giant of the sky. Rosendahl looked down with
fond memories of the gray buildings where he had
been stationed just prior to entering LTA training
eight years earlier. The *Los Angeles* was following
the *Akron* on this trip, and the midshipmen sighted
her five miles astern of *Akron*.

By 10:15 a.m. the *Akron* was over the Washington Navy Yard, and since Admiral Moffett was
aboard the airship, the Yard fired a salute to him.
The *Los Angeles* had joined up closer and after the
ships took their aerial tour of the nation's capital,
they went on to Baltimore, at 11:40 a.m. being
viewed by visitors to Fort McHenry, birthplace of
the national anthem.

They reached Elkton, Md., where couples
wishing instant marriage ceremonies looked up in
wonder at the immense ships before heading on
their honeymoons. A minute after noon *Akron*
reached Wilmington and six minutes later she overflew Philadelphia, where sightseers at the Liberty
Bell admired the ships of the sky. At 1:13 p.m.
they circled Trenton. At sunset they landed back
at Lakehurst.

On Monday, November 9, the ship made a local
flight with a record-making 207 persons aboard.
The idea was to demonstrate how the airship could
airlift a sizeable number of military personnel for
an emergency.

On one of the early flights in November the
aviation editor of the *Washington Daily News* took
a flight on the *Akron*. He was Ernie Pyle, of slight
stature, high forehead and thinning red hair, but a
giant at the typewriter. He was a master at sim-
plifying a complex subject, and he filed a three-
part series of articles telling the public about life
aboard the world's largest "dirigible." His descrip-
tion of the fins was masterful in its simplicity:

"From the rear end of the cat-walk, one climbs
back into the upper vertical fin. This corresponding
fin on an airplane is about the size of a table top
and as thick as your hand.

"But on the *Akron* it is as high as a six-story
building and as wide as your living room (proba-

bly). The Navy once considered putting the crew's quarters in the lower fin, and would have except that the weight would have upset the ship's balance.

"To get to the lower fin you crawl down a series of skeleton ladders. Although the fin is really a very small part of the whole dirigible, yet it is so big you could set up housekeeping in it."

Pyle's write-up went on to extol the virtues of the lower fin as a fine point for sight-seeing, if one is not addicted to air sickness.

"When the *Akron* hits a bump, the nose goes down and the tail goes up, and if you're in the tail you go up several hundred feet sometimes. *And the whole fin shivers and shakes as though it would fall off.* (Italics are not by Pyle, but by the author.)

Pyle noted that the air was always fresh and pure throughout the ship. Fresh air blew freely through the windows, which were not visible from the ground but were on all sides of the airship. He likened his ride to one in an ocean liner rather than in a plane.

"In rough air, the nose simply goes up or down, very slowly. At the bottom of a long pitch, when passengers are bracing to keep their chairs from sliding along the floor, the dirigible hangs there at an angle seemingly interminably, before she starts coming back.

"The sensation is exactly the same as on a steamship when she goes down into a deep trough."

In November some of the new men came to join the crew. Among them were Tony Frank Swidersky, Seaman First Class who would learn to be an elevator man, and Lt. Daniel Ward Harrigan, who was to head the hook-on pilot contingent. Six chairs were placed in the control car, along with one parachute for use in emergency mooring situations where a man could be dropped in advance if necessary to instruct the ground handling force. Two aircraft mechanics were busy installing a radio direction finder at frame 178, while others were repairing engines five and six and plugging in oil heaters on all engines. One of the crew put his foot through the outer cover at frame 170 and the ship's riggers made the necessary repair.

Lt. Ward Harrigan was a tall, effervescent pilot who set about doing liaison with the aircraft manufacturer producing the Curtiss F9C2. An Academy graduate of the class of 1922, he had palled at being an instructor and had put in for the more

A rigger climbs the ladder leading to the top keel walkway. As he climbs, the ladder is in reversed position to facilitate passage. *J. Christian Fenger photo.*

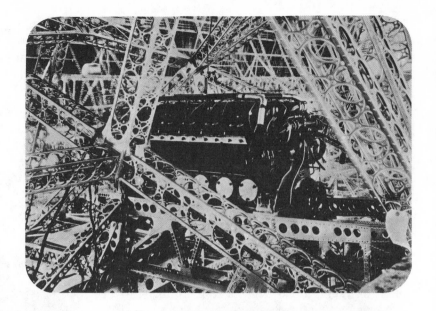

At right: one of the *Akron's* eight Maybach 12-cylinder engines. Each developes 560 h.p. at 1,6000 r.p.m., Below, airship crewmen oil the 60 degree V-type engine. Each engine has a dry weight of 2,600 pounds. The airship normally carries 2,400 pounds of oil and 110,000 pounds of fuel.
Official U.S. Navy photos.

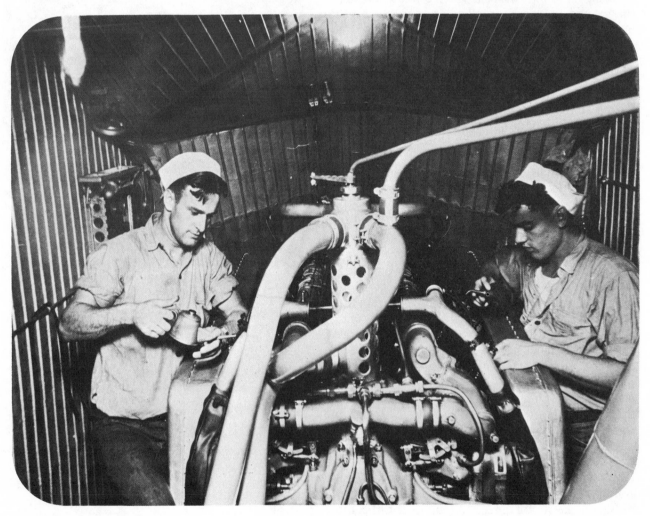

challenging job of testing the new scouting planes that would make the *Akron* the Navy's first flying aircraft carrier, if one did not count the experimental attachments to the *Los Angeles,* on which the planes could not be drawn up into the belly of the mother ship. His job was to be an uphill one, because LCdr. Rosendahl saw the airship as primarily its own scout and the full potential of the hook-ons would take several years to take hold. Of a bubbling, "can-do" personality, Harrigan became a popular officer with the crew and his associates.

November flights took the airship to Norfolk on the 10th and to Akron and Cleveland on the 11th. The return from Pittsburgh was via Buffalo, Niagara Falls, Schenectady, Rhinebeck and Poughkeepsie. On the 23rd the *Akron* flew to Portland, Maine, returning the next day to overfly the New York area, on the 24th overflying Jones Beach, Fire Island and arriving at Lakehurst at 3:30 p.m.

In December, several flights were taken off the Jersey coast and in the middle of the month, Admiral Moffett's flag was flown as the ship visited Philadelphia, Chester, Conowingo Dam, Baltimore, Washington, Richmond and on to Louisville. The next day, Dec. 17, they flew to Cincinnati and at 7:30 a.m. the *Akron* was over Caldwell, Ohio. LCdr. Rosendahl pointed out the Nichols farm west of that town where in 1925 the *Shenandoah's* bow, with half a dozen others aboard beside Rosendahl, was brought down successfully. A few miles north of Caldwell, he overflew the Davis farm where other sections of the ill-fated *Shenandoah* came to rest. By the time they reached Richmond, there was heavy rain at 9:20 p.m. and visibility was almost zero. By 3 a.m. they were over Warrenton, Va. and as day broke the ship was completely surrounded by stratus clouds. No planes were flying, but the airship was safely flown to Lakehurst where at 6:06 p.m. the bow of the ship crossed the sill of the hangar.

Over the Christmas holidays 28 men went on leave including Augie Quernheim, ACMM, Bill Boswell, CBM, former *Shenandoah* crewmen, and the *Akron's* new chief radio man, Robert W. Copeland. After their five day respite, a similar number of crewmen took leave.

January 4, 1932 the *Akron* flew to New York City. Then on the 9th, she went south to Raleigh and out into the Atlantic, where she sighted destroyers in a fleet exercise. On Sunday, January 17 at 7:30 a.m. she moored for the first time to the shipborne mast of the *Patoka* at Plantation Flats. While the mast crew was disconnecting the pendant and main mooring wire, the ship's cone disconnected because the cup lugs were not locked. With a loud "snap" the lugs sheared off while the cone was seated in the cup. The *Akron* began to rise, carrying the yaw guys with it. Recommendations were made upon return to correct the procedure for the next shipboard mooring.

Tuesday morning, February 22 dawned with wintry skies and Lt. Charles Roland, mooring officer, knew he had a busy day ahead of him as he wiped the sleep from his eyes. Both the *Los Angeles* and the *Akron* were slated to fly, the latter to carry the House Naval Affairs Committee aloft. At 8:15 a.m. he called Cdr. Rosendahl and informed him the equipment was in place to undock the older airship first. Rosendahl quickly told Roland that the *Akron* should come out of the hangar first.

"It will take an hour to make ready for the *Akron,*" Roland said over the phone.

"Cut it to a half-hour," Rosendahl said. "We want to get her out before the wind picks up."

In the aerologist's office, Lt. Charles Maguire made his early morning forecast. Surface winds were 10-12 miles an hour, fluctuating from northwest and northeast. Peering outside, he saw clouds starting to break, the ceiling was lifting and visibility improving. Maguire briefed both Captain Fred Berry of the *Los Angeles* and Captain Rosendahl that the wind would pick up to 25-30 knots. A special pilot balloon ascent was completed at 8:30 a.m., indicating light winds for the present, but the sooner out of the hangar the better.

At 9:10 a.m. the diminutive figure of Lt. Anthony Danis appeared. Danis looked over the 8 a.m. map, then went to Rosendahl to confirm Maguire's report. Rosendahl wanted the ship out before the wind would hit the vast exposed surface area with a strong quartering wind.

The ship was moving out slowly into the quartering wind, heading stern first. Lt. Calvin Bolster (CC) connected the ship to the stern-beam and secured it in the center of the floating support for the fin. He showed a green flag to LCdr. Herbert Wiley. Bolster realized the wind was picking up, giving a large side load, more than two-thirds of the

Damage in this stern handling accident to the *Akron* totals $98,450 in repairs necessary and $3,000
to handling equipment. Rear Admiral William Moffett (in the distance, by the rail and near the struts)
walks away from the scene which delayed the House Naval Affairs Committee's flight.
National Archives photo.

total side force being taken up by the stern handling gear that he had helped design. The ship was secured at the bow to a mooring mast pushed by a locomotive at one mile an hour speed.

A third of the way out of the hangar, Lt. Roland saw the wind was sailing the bow into the hangar. The locomotive was slipping on the rails, then stopped. The engineer applied sand to the rails. The pushing began again, with more speed, now making about three miles an hour. Near the stern, at frame 35, two pendants with handling lines were manned by 30 men on each pendant. The weight of the two groups would steady the ship while it was disconnected from the beam.

LCdr. Wiley followed the stern beam, 20 feet behind it. He ordered the "X" frames put on to reinforce the after fin. When the speed of the mast and movement of the ship decreased, he ordered. "Speed it up."

Forward, in the control car, Chief Radioman Bob Copeland was at the telephone switchboard. Wiley noted the rudder was heading right, and he questioned the wisdom of having the large surface in the extreme starboard position. Somehow, the order was received not as a question from the talker to whom Wiley relayed the message. Copeland heard an order, "Hard right rudder." "Hard right rudder?"

"Yes, hard right," the talker said over the telephone.

LCdr. Bert Rodgers, senior engineering officer, called rigger Joe Zimkus up from the keel to assist Boatswain's Mate 2nd Class Pascal Jackson on the rudder wheel. On the port side of the control car, Quartermaster 1st Class Ralph Stine kept the elevators amidships.

After an interval, Wiley sent a new order forward through the talker: "Bring the rudder amidships!"

To carry out the order required full force by Jackson and Zimkus, The full force of the rising wind made Rodgers fear that the rudder controls might carry away.

Lt. Roland Mayer was on the port side of the control car, managing the ballast. When the car reached the hangar door, Mayer heard a sharp sound like a cable snapping.

In the stern, a rigger inside the ship called, "Major controls for the upper rudder at frame 17½ have carried away!"

The tow pendant from frame 0-35 on the port side carried away, and the ship listed to starboard nine degrees. With the bridle at frame 0 suddenly detached, lines ran recklessly through the blocks.

"Look out for the wires," yelled LCdr. Wiley. His first impulse was to run and board the ship in the event she took to the air. The snapping wires stopped his passage.

Lt. Mayer also thought the ship might take off. He saw Cdr. Rosendahl on the ground abreast of the car, and reported the rudder control failure.

"Go aft and investigate," said Rosendahl quickly. Mayer ran down the starboard catwalk toward the stern.

To LCdr. Bert Rodgers, the sound seemed to come from the elevator wheel cable where they were exposed to view in the navigator's compartment to the rear of the car. Reaching the location, Mayer met Lt. Morgan Redfield. Neither he nor Lt. George Campbell, in the gun room, could pinpoint the trouble.

Lt. Bob Sayre, Assistant Mooring Officer, had been concentrating on the movement of the starboard elevator as the wind from port side pushed the ship into a list, rolling to starboard. Suddenly he saw the joint at frame 0, the first longeron on the port side, carry away.

Stocky LCdr. Jess Kenworthy saw two men lying on the ground, struck by failing material and wires. He picked up Lt. Cal Bolster, who staggered from a bleeding head wound. On the other side, Machinist's Mate 2nd Class Frank Gonsior also was a casualty.

Lt. Mayer, as he ran along the starboard gangway, was at engine car 1 when he heard the crashing and breaking of structure. Looking out, he saw the ship sweeping across the field. Thinking the ship was taking off, he ran back to the control car. He dropped ballast to take care of the static condition of the ship aft. Then, out the port window, he saw the ship was 40 feet in the air, swinging rapidly aft. The fin had risen twice and grounded before pointing into the wind bedeviling the ship from the north.

Mayer went to the stern again. The noise to him had come from the rudder control wheel itself, as if a chain was jumping a sprocket well. When he talked to Coxswain Barnhart, who had reported from frame 17' that the controls had carried away, he realized why Barnhart had come to that conclusion. What he had seen was slack on the cable, which dropped from its original position to near

Sailors standing on girders in the lower fin of the *Akron* look down toward the emergency control station.
National Archives photo.

the walkway girder.

A maximum gust of wind at 26 miles an hour had registered on the anemometer at 9:43 a.m.

Seaman 1st Class Leo Gentile was only two feet from the port longitudinal which gave way at frame 0. Just before, he felt a quiver in the fin. After that, everything broke loose.

Another sailor was a foot-and-a-half from Gentile, Ralph Engler heard a clattering of wires in the fin when the longitudinal broke. He went from the port window to the ladder, looked down into the fin just before the joint failed.

"Hold on, that's all we can do," Englar said to Gentile.

Coxswain Francis Donovan was at frame 17½ in the upper part of the fin. He heard the whole fin groan as the ship moved out. It was laboring before the longitudinal gave. He found himself down at the bottom of the car, his feet thrown out. When the ship first hit, he had somehow climbed down. After it blew halfway around the mooring out circle, he was thrown out backward to the windward side and onto the ground.

The damage after inspection by Cdr. Sydney Kraus, manager of the Naval Aircraft Factory in Philadelphia, came to $98,450 to the ship and $3,000 to the handling equipment. The lower third of the ship's girders at the stern were smashed. In frame 0, 30 structural members were fractured or buckled, requiring replacement. At frame 17½ there were 52 broken members. On the port side at frame 35 aft 90 members were damaged; to starboard 105 had to be replaced. A thousand wires necessary to the integrity of the ship's structure had to be tensioned and respliced. Gas cells 1 and 2 had very large tears, and 80 per cent of the lower fin's cover had to be replaced. Practically all of the outer cover aft of frame 35 had to be removed and replaced. No one was held responsible. The stern was detached due to material casualty.

On April 28, with LCdr. Rosendahl away on emergency leave, LCdr. Wiley took the ship to New York on a post repair flight. The Secretary of the Navy and Admiral Moffett were passengers and observed tests of new hook-on gear and trial of the observation basket. Another post-repair flight took place on May 3rd, when a full-power run was made under supervision of the Board of Inspection and Survey. Lt. Harrigan made a number of hook-ons and the plane was hoisted into the airship. The ship's radio direction finder also was calibrated on the flight, and the flight which began at 6:12 a.m. ended with mooring out at Lakehurst at 8:38 p.m. The next day the House Naval Affairs Committee went along to watch further plane handling tests. The tests indicated a need to beef-up portions of the airplane handling gear, and the work was rushed to completion for the upcoming West Coast cruise.

On Sunday May 8, the *Akron* left the air station at 5:55 a.m., leaving behind the observation basket, which needed further refinement. Only one fighting plane, the *XF9C* No. 8731 had been delivered. This plane and the *N2Y* were selected to join up with the Akron for the trip. Aboard were 13 officers and 63 enlisted men, ten of whom were in training. Cdr. Alger H. Dresel, under orders to take command upon completion of the cruise, was aboard as the ship took off with a ceiling of only 600 feet. At 7:20 a.m., over Barnegat Bay, the airplanes hooked on and were housed, the two officers—Lts. Harrigan and Howard Young—bringing the total personnel aboard to 80.

The airship headed for Cape Hatteras and then swung to a southwesterly course. By 11:45 a.m. she was over Norfolk; Raleigh, 2:45 p.m.; Augusta, Ga. at 8:15 p.m.; Mobile at 4:30 a.m. May 9th and New Orleans at 7:45 a.m. as headwinds kept groundspeed at about 49 knots. For two hours out of New Orleans, low clouds gave nearly zero visibility. Headwinds prevailed as the big ship overflew Beaumont, Texas at 1:14 p.m., followed by Port Arthur, Galveston and Houston at 3:50 p.m. The navigator's track indicated crossing the mountains west of El Paso at the lowest point to conserve helium. Northwest Texas was full of thunderstorms, while the El Paso route had only widely scattered storms.

At 5:05 p.m. a service fuel tank at frame 47.5 on the port side suddenly opened up an inch above a welded seam. Fifteen hundred pounds of gasoline was dumped into the ship.

"Stop all engines but number seven," Rosendahl ordered, and the deck officer relayed the order over the telegraph system. While the fumes were being vented, the smell was evident in the control car far forward of where the tank had split. In an hour the weather became thick to westward. Rosendahl was watching a cloud on the starboard bow.

"It looks as if it highly charged," the captain observed to Cdr. Dresel.

A petty officer enters an engine room on the port side using the narrow walkway.
National Archives photo.

A three-quarters bow view of the *Akron* moored to the mast at Sunnyvale, California, after having made an emergency landing at Camp Kearny while en route. Vertical units above propellers are for water recovery from gasoline burned in flight to keep weight balanced.
Official U.S. Navy photo.

"Look at that one," Dresel said, pointing to an apparently harmless cloud on the port bow. As he spoke, a terrific bolt of lightning struck the ground from the innocent-looking cloud.

Soon, in the vicinity of San Antonio lightning was more intense from several storms. Arriving at that city at 8 p.m., thunderstorms to the west and southwest caused Rosendahl to detour to the northwest.

"We'll take her to Fort Worth-El Paso Airway if we have to," Rosendahl told Dresel.

At 10:25 p.m. around San Angelo, large and intense thunderstorms blocked the Akron's progress. Rosendahl decided to heave to and use the airway beacon of the airport there to keep position. After five hours awaiting the storm's abatement, the Akron received a message from the commandant of Randolph Field, offering a civilian ground crew to make an emergency landing to wait out the weather.

The normal flashing of the ship's navigation lights while it was hove-to over the airport had been mistaken for distress signals. Rosendahl thanked the Army Air Corps for the invitation, but expressed no interest in landing.

As the stormy night pressed on, the thunderstorms covered the western horizon. The airship was making 60 knots airspeed just to keep heading into the wind and to avoid being drawn into the boiling clouds around her. The blinding lightning kept up throughout the night. The radio antennae were housed and radio communication was out except for high frequency contact with Navy radio in Washington. The storms finally subsided with daylight and at 7:45 a.m. the ship was over Langtry, Texas in low broken clouds. Rosendahl headed the ship for the pass at Alpine, increasing altitude to 4,500 feet, but the clouds again closed in and he made a 180 degree change in course. Two hours later, he decided to follow the Pecos river northward for a try at the Van Horn pass. At 12:38 p.m. it was still raining, with squalls and low clouds, and the Akron followed the Southern Pacific Railroad to the pass, but had to heave to at 5,000 feet in zero visibility. After several aborted attempts, the ship reached 6,800 feet, and the sonic altimeter or Echolot showed the ground was 1,500 feet below. At last, by 6:02 p.m. patches of blue sky appeared and the ship broke out into dazzling sunlight in sight of Van Horn. Only a few minutes before she had been feeling her way in blinding fog. A tower-

ing thunderstrom cloud was on the port hand.

Ten miles short of El Paso, once the pass was negotiated, the air became smooth, but only for a short while. Violent turbulence followed. Over the city a peculiar haze like a thin fog enveloped the area.

"A mild sandstorm is in progress," the aerological officer notified Rosendahl. The news had come from the Department of Commerce radio there. The northerly winds were blowing sand into the control car even as he read the dispatch at 5,500 feet!

Rosendahl looked down at the airport below, where a formation of planes was about to take off. The leader got into the air, bounced around in the turbulence, turned around and landed. The others did not follow, having seen their leader rock and roll almost to a crash. The Akron ran eastward but could not outrun the storm. Vertical currents carried the ship up or down at 480 feet per minute.

The ship then resumed course westward, using full speed to go through the pass. Once through, despite strong downcurrents, the ship was soon in smoother air on a clear, starlit night. Another sudden sand storm sprung up at 8:05 p.m. and lasted for 20 minutes. The hot air made the ship heavy and full speed was necessary again to control the ship in the rough air.

As they proceeded to Douglas, Tucson, and Phoenix the night was over and they reached Yuma at 6:30 a.m. The terrific straining and motion of the ship in the sand storms opened up an eight-inch hole in no. 6 gas cell. Riggers hastily repaired it.

All the running at high speed during the storms had depleted the fuel supply, along with slow speed while surrounded by thunderstorms. Rosendahl had to decide whether to risk the longer leg to Sunnyvale or to make a stop at Camp Kearney to refuel. The former location near San Francisco could be plagued by fog, which would require burning more fuel before mooring. The Sunnyvale crew was no more experienced at mooring than the one at Camp Kearney. Winds of from 15-20 knots were forecast for the route between San Diego and San Francisco. Rosendahl opted for Camp Kearney, whence he could cast off after refueling and join the Fleet Sortie from San Francisco a day later to participate in exercises.

At 8 a.m. May 11 the ship arrived over San Diego with only 16,090 pounds of fuel left. Nearby Camp Kearney was shrouded in fog. Rosendahl

Apprentice Seaman Charles M. "Bud" Cowart, aboard the *Akron*. The 18-year old sailor's introduction to airships provides a spine-tingling aerial ride while dangling below the *Akron* on a trail line.
Official U.S. Navy photo.

ordered the hook-on planes to go down through breaks in the fog. At 8:37 a.m., the *N2Y* plane landed Lt. Scott E. Peck so he could assist in the mooring. The Curtiss *XF9C-2* followed. Then the airship proceeded seaward, diving through the fog and came out at 1,200 feet in the clear. The ship rushed to make the landing at Camp Kearney before the sun's heat would cause turbulent air. At 10:55 a.m. the trail ropes were dropped, but the inexperienced ground crew of recruits did not grab the lines, even though the coils landed near the landing flag. The *Akron* then circled the field, but proved too high for contact and had to circle again. The "boots" grabbed the lines and the main mooring cable was run out and connected to the mast cable at 11:31 a.m.

Rosendahl knew he had a problem in making the landing. Camp Kearney was on a plateau surrounded by ravines and gullies. Only scrubby brush at intervals dotted the dusty surface. Dust whirls and convection currents would increase after the sun increased the thermals. Between the plateau and the mountains eastward, the contour rose rapidly and unevenly, making the ship bump in the approach at slow airspeed. Air density differences would make for instant buoyancy changes. At the point where the trail ropes normally would be dropped, the tail of the ship projected out over a deep canyon. The air under the broken fog had its own temperature differences and bumpiness.

The mooring equipment at Camp Kearney featured a main winch that had been used to moor the *Shenandoah* at North Island in 1924, when Rosendahl was navigator. The gasoline-driven winch had a top hauling-in speed of only 80 feet per minute at constant speed. Total pull was 1,800 pounds, inadequate for a ship of the *Akron's* size. Temperature at the mast was 75 degrees, but in a few minutes it changed to 9 degrees cooler. A temporary loss of buoyancy of about four per cent of the gross lift occurred.

With little airspeed, the ship was difficult to control in the gusts and yawed in various directions. Four engines were going full speed downward, yet the ship became more buoyant nevertheless. The slow speed of the main winch made the near vertical angle of the trail ropes even more vertical.

"Open helium valves full," Rosendahl ordered.

The attempt to reduce buoyancy failed. The ship now inclined more than 20 degrees.

The deck officer was then instructed to warn the mooring parties and Lt. Peck to stand by to cut the main wire and let go everything.

Despite the downward thrust of four props and unstinted valving of helium, the airship's angle grew to more than 25 degrees—off the inclinometer in the control car. Complicating matters further, valves in several water ballast bags tripped themselves and 3,000 pounds of water were dumped on those below, aggravating the inclination. The weak mast main mooring winch began slipping.

The ship's engines stopped as the inclination cut off their fuel supply.

"Free flight is our only answer," said Rosendahl.

"Cut the main wire," the deck officer relayed by megaphone.

Lt. Peck, at the mast, found himself alone to cut the wire. His assistant had "abandoned ship," sliding down a mast guy to the ground. Peck could not cut the 7/8″ steel mooring cable alone. He dropped the bolt clippers to the foot of the mast and told those below to cut the main wire there.

For Oklahoma-born Apprentice Seaman Charles M. Cowart, known as "Bud" to his shipmates at the Naval Training Station, the morning which began at 5:30 a.m. was getting to be a long one. A total of 122 men were assigned to help bring their first airship down, half of them brought in from the air station at San Diego at breakfast time. During the three abortive attempts to land the ship, the group had become tired from running over the rough terrain after the ship's lines.

The 18-year old Cowart and the others received brief instruction on landing procedures.

"When they throw down the lines and they are attached to our cable," an officer said, "grab a toggle line and run at right angles to the ship."

Cowart joined the group of sailors on the starboard spider hook. The strain on the lines was great.

Lt. Scott Peck continued to give instructions to the recruits. "Keep her from hitting the ground. Be speedy in hooking on the lines and get a strain on them."

Lt. Caleb Coatsworth, Jr., from San Diego, was in charge of preparation, since he was a qualified blimp pilot. The original plan had been to send an officer and two experienced men to Kearney in the event of the landing, but anticipating a landing at San Diego, the men had not arrived.

Lt. (jg) J. F. Addoms, supervising the port trail

The two recruits who lost their lives in the aborted landing of the *Akron* could not improve their precarious grip on the spider lines and fell to their deaths from less than 200 feet.
Navy Dept. photo in the National Archives.

line on the other side of Cowart's group, instructed the men to be wary of a sudden rise in the airship.

"When your feet leave the ground, let go of the toggles," Addoms yelled over the din of the engines rumbling above.

Lt. (jg) Ward Harrigan, the hook-on pilot who brought himself and Lt. Peck down, was in charge of the port and starboard trail rope groups. After the first unsuccessful approach, Peck ordered Lt. Coatsworth down from the mast to assist Harrigan, who was still a student in Lighter-Than-Air but the senior heavier-than-air pilot of the ship.

The ship was tugging at the lines to which the sailors clung fiercely.

"Put all your weight on it," a heavy-set officer yelled at the men. Responding, some tried to climb up in the ropes. Suddenly, the rectangular ring to which the toggle lines of the port group were secured snapped apart at a weld point.

Seaman 2nd Class C. J. Toland went with others from the port line to the starboard group and grabbed hold. With him were Aviation Carpenter's Mate Harold Edsal, Apprentice Seamen Nigel Merton Henton and D. G. Walkup. Edsal heard another order.

"Get on top and put your weight on her!"

Edsal jumped over the men on the outside lines, climbed to an upper toggle and sat on it, next to "Bud" Cowart. Toland was nearby, and talked to Edsal.

"Don't let her get away," Toland remarked.

Henton and Edsal, sensing that the ship might rise at any moment, slid down from the upper toggles to the lowest ones in order to get off quickly. Cowart remained on the upper toggle.

Cowart saw the recruits below barely had their toes on the ground. Henton and Edsal were hanging at arms length to be near the ground. Suddenly the ship rose into the air. The men below dropped off like flies.

"Let go!" yelled Lts. Harrigan and Coatsworth simultaneously.

The ship was ascending at 400 feet per minute. Cowart watched Seaman D. G. Walkup let go from fifteen feet above the underbrush. He dislocated his elbow. From twenty feet, Seaman Toland let go, but seemed to be unhurt. Edsal and Henton, clinging at arms length, held on.

Henton was trying to better his grip on the stick. He let go with his left hand to climb up but somehow slipped. Edsal also was trying valiantly to climb. At a hundred feet, Edsal slipped off and hurtled to the ground. Cowart watched in horror as Edsal fell. Not wanting to see more, Cowart looked up at the behemoth carrying him ever upward.

Lt. Coatsworth watched the hurtling recruit and tried to attract the attention of the two corpsmen and doctor on duty.

Within half-a-minute, Henton reached 200 feet. He, too, slipped off—just before Edsal struck. Henton was fighting all the way down. He bounced four feet in the air, turned over and came to rest on his stomach.

When the doctor, Lt. (jg) James Sapero, and the corpsmen reached the two men, there was nothing they could do. Both had died instantly from multiple extreme injuries.

Cowart could hear that the men in the airship were yelling to him. He had a good hold on the 3½ inch thick manila line and toggles formed a tiny boatswain's seat. He held on as the ship kept circling the area at 1,500 feet altitude.

A dozen men in the airship under Lt. Roland Mayer's direction started hauling Cowart slowly up to the open hatch. Mayer, a Construction Corps officer who had stayed in after the war and had more time in lighter-than-air than anyone in the Navy, was the man airshipmen called upon in emergencies. He had served with Rosendahl when both were lieutenants in the early days at Lakehurst. Quiet and unassuming, Mayer again was helping the captain out of a messy situation.

After a half-hour had passed since takeoff, the man entwined in the rope yelled up to the men looking down at him through the hatch:

"When are you going to land me?" Cowart asked. It was the first sign of activity on his part.

"Hang on, son," Lt. Mayer yelled. "It may take an hour more, so keep wrapped in those toggles and lines 'til we get you up here."

Others joined in with words of encouragement as the minutes went slowly by and the dangling recruit's line was inched upwards.

At one point the greasy 7/8" thick steel cable dangling from the bow swung near him. That main mooring cable was a thousand feet in length, and couldn't be hauled in because the main mooring winch drum was being used to pull up Cowart.

The big cable came Cowart's way again.

"Do you want me to slide down that cable to the ground?" Cowart asked those above.

Perspiring from working their makeshift rig to

Apprentice Seaman C. M. "Bud" Cowart keeps a firm hold on the toggles of a trail line for two hours after being carried aloft in an aborted landing attempt at Camp Kearney near San Diego, California.
Navy Dept. photo in the National Archives.

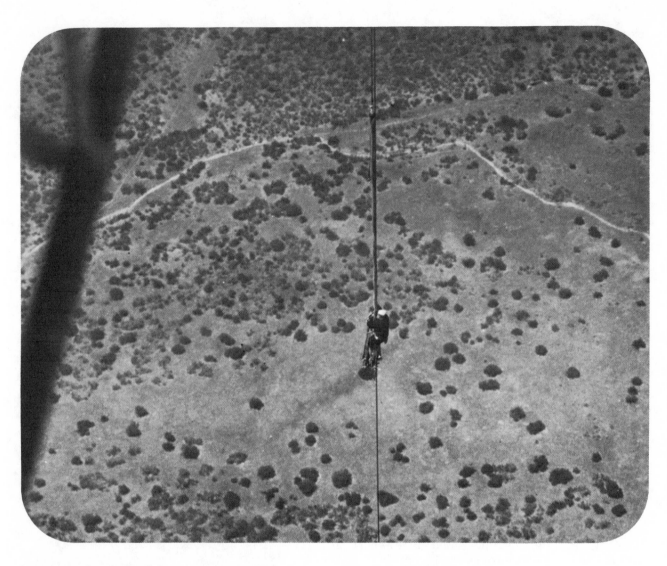

Apprentice Seaman "Bud" Cowart perches himself atop a nest of toggles on one of the *Akron's* trail lines. After the airship aborts her landing at Camp Kearney May 11, 1931, he is able to hold on for two hours.
Navy Dept. photo in the National Archives.

haul him in, the crew felt they were too near pulling him aboard to risk having him slip off now.

"Hold fast," Mayer yelled, "It won't be long—we don't want to lose you!"

Dick "Lucky" Deal then volunteered to shinny down the main cable and fasten an auxiliary line to Cowart. His offer was refused. Thirty times Lt. Mayer's group had thrown a stopper on the line as it entered the ship. They cut the thick line from the small winch and began again. After two long hours, they brought Cowart to the hatch.

Cowart's hand was grasped by the rescuers and he was hauled aboard. Mayer patted him warmly on the shoulders. Cowart showed no sign of shock. He announced that he was attached to the Naval Training Station at San Diego and had been detailed to Camp Kearney for the landing party.

Lt. Mayer took him to meet the captain before sending the recruit off to wash and have some food in the crew's quarters.

The *Akron* continued to cruise in the vicinity until sunset, when the landing at Camp Kearney was made at 6:58 p.m., with fog quickly setting in. While the mooring was underway, several hundred feet of slack had been hauled in when the clutch between the engine and winch froze fast. The ground handlers quickly switched to using hand gear to complete hauling down the ship. Connections to put fuel and water aboard from the mast were not ready, nor was the stern taxying device fitted to attach it to the ship's stern. The green crew finally installed the connections and by 10 p.m. the *Akron* was in a safe riding condition.

A crowd of several hundred automobiles that had been driven to park near the mooring site was ordered away by a company of marines. Allowing the spectators to remain would have jeopardized the safety of the ship.

The next morning, May 12, fueling was begun to replace that burned, but since considerable helium had been valved, Rosendahl ordered the two airplanes, their pilots and ten enlisted men to go to Sunnyvalle separately. The weight saved allowed taking on their weight in fuel. No helium was available at Camp Kearney.

Before noon the ship was unmoored and soon was flying north, passing Long Beach at 1:35 p.m. and Los Angeles at 2:02 p.m. Reaching Point Conception at 6:15 p.m., the surface was covered by fog as it had been all afternoon. Rosendahl then ordered the ship to drive down through the fog,

where at 700 feet the fog was now overhead. Half-an-hour after midnight the *Akron* reached San Francisco. She cruised in the area awaiting sunrise, but when it came the fog completely obscured the surface. She made a try to go through the Golden Gate, following the lightship and main ship channel buoys from 700 feet, but the fog cut her off again. By 6:35 a.m. the fog's density decreased at the bay's lower end. At 9:30 a.m. the ship approached to land, but the fog ceiling was still low and under it the air was gusty and turbulent. A landing was not in the cards for Rosendahl, since the ship was now statically light and the hangar near the mast made it unwise to try to control the ship in the tight quarters under the conditions.

The ship then cruised in the Bay area and at 7:06 p.m. *Akron* was finally moored without difficulty.

Lt. Roland Mayer then sent riggers to inspect the ship following completion of the transcontinental trip. They found several holes in cells more than a foot long made during the San Diego mooring attempt. When Mayer saw two broken intermediate girders which a rigger pointed out, he ordered them to put wooden splints over them for a temporary repair. "Doctor Mayer" was no stranger to splinting broken girders—he had done the same thing as far back as nine years earlier, when the *Shenandoah* made her first overnight flight to St. Louis.

Mayer also ordered the ship's company to make repairs on the water recovery panels on the side of the *Akron*. Removing unwanted carbon was a task as unpopular as was "pots and pans" duty to Army kitchen police!

On May 13 LCdr. Rosendahl flew to San Pedro to confer with the Commander-in-Chief of the U.S. Fleet. A tentative schedule was laid down for the *Akron*. She would moor to the *Patoka* in the bay, with press representatives aboard the converted oil tanker. A score of reporters would be carried on a flight over the Stockton-Sacramento-Vallejo area. A high altitude flight to Bakersfield down the San Joaquin Valley would be followed by a non-stop flight to Washington and Oregon points first overflown by the *Shenandoah* in October 1924. Return to Lakehurst was scheduled for the end of the month.

The schedule was flown as planned. High winds on the trip to Bremerton kept ground speed down to 16 knots. On her return, *Akron* was invited to participate in tactical exercises with the Scouting Force through June 3rd. The original schedule to leave the end of May was to avoid the increasing frequency of thunderstorms of summer, but Rosendahl jumped at the chance to participate.

His ship had been plagued with operating difficulties that first year. On this expedition, the Sunnyvale facility was not completed. The arrival at Camp Kearney saw the ship with five-sixths of her fuel burned off and only one-sixth left, and she had lost considerable helium.

As 1932 began, she was not ready for her first scouting exercise. The Naval Aircraft Factory had not completed the new trapeze, even though it had cannibalized the trapeze used on the *Los Angeles* for experimental hook-ons. It had finally been de-

livered in February, but the damage to the lower fin a few weeks later made it impossible to do any hook-ons until just prior to leaving for the West Coast trip.

True, in her mid-winter Scouting Force exercise down to the Bahamas she had gone 3,000 miles in three days, encountering in the north severe snow and icing conditions so that over Baltimore at one point she carried eight tons of ice. Over the Atlantic she discovered a cruiser and a dozen destroyers, but missed some destroyers which themselves sighted the airship. Adverse remarks had come from Vice Adm. Willard of the Scouting Forces.

Rosendahl was now anxious to make a good showing in the exercise on the West Coast.

An ususual close-up of the control car of the *Akron* as the airship flies over the desert on her West Coast flight, the rudder man clearly visible as a freight train rolls along below.
National Archives photo.

CHAPTER SIX

Scouting the Enemy

Scouting exercises on the west coast commenced June 1, with the *Akron* a member of the Green force opposing a White force of cruisers and destroyer screen. Captain Rosendahl knew he had a difficult proposition to locate the enemy, which had a choice of two destinations out over the Pacific. He drew limiting ellipses and began a retiring search curve at the north and started there, heading southward at a thousand feet. Visibility varied from zero to up to 35 miles as the big ship cruised along, wary of being spotted first by the Whites.

Every hour Rosendahl changed the course. Making about 68 knots with a good tail wind, the airship at noon spotted a number of friendly Green vessels heading northward on an independent search.

The next day, at 3:21 p.m. the airship sighted the White force on the horizon some 30 nautical miles away. Maneuvering to keep out of gun range, Rosendahl noted two seaplanes being launched despite the rough seas. The pair of slow scouting aircraft reached the *Akron* and Rosendahl felt the airship could easily have repelled them with her own 50-caliber machine guns. By 8 p.m., the *Akron* maneuvered in the probable enemy area, feeling they were undoubtedly heading for the southern destination. The enemy was lost in the airship's effort to keep out of gun range and due to poor visibility.

Twenty-four hours after the first sighting, also in midafternoon, the *Akron* again picked up the main body of the White force. The cruisers deployed immediately to launch planes. *Akron* kept the sun gauge, hiding behind its glow, and making what use she could of thin and broken clouds for concealment. At 3:27 p.m. two seaplanes again attacked the *Akron*.

Rosendahl then brought the *Akron* out of the clouds and took position astern of the enemy, which he soon realized was a faulty decision. Reaching the more broken clouds near the White force, the *Akron* was suddenly attacked by five planes of the enemy.

Rosendahl, pacing the floor of the control car, looked displeased as he remarked to Cdr. Dresel, his prospective relief:

"If we had held our original course, they never would have found us!"

"That's right," Dresel replied. "They didn't have much search time available."

At 4:10 p.m., the *Akron* again sighted the White force, keeping it in sight from 20 miles distance, and still in the sun gauge. The cruisers were having difficulty recovering their planes, one of which sank in the choppy seas and another was seriously damaged before finally being hauled aboard her cruiser. If the Green ships had been on the scene they might have done damage to the White ships, which were heading in all directions and generating considerable smoke.

Shortly before sunset that June 4, 1932, the *Akron* received orders to discontinue the exercise. Rosendahl felt the airship had done well, considering she was the only *aerial* scout while most other craft searched in multiples. In most occasions, the airship sighted the surface craft several minutes before she herself was sighted. He felt that if experimentation on camouflage could be undertaken, the airship might have even more of an advantage. In a real war, he doubted that a surface force seeking to find and destroy an enemy would launch observation planes in perilous seas to attack an airship scout. Having radioed the location of the

With Admiral Moffett's flag flying and a hook-on plane on the trapeze, the *Akron* flies over San Francisco with the Golden Gate to the west.
National Air and Space Museum photo.

enemy ships, even destruction of the airship with the comparatively small loss of life would have an acceptable cost. If gas cells were punctured, the *Akron* could be repaired in flight. Hydrogen-filled zeppelins in World War I with up to three cells deflated not only remained afloat but even returned home. A bombing attack could of course cut controls or hit fuel tanks, but the airship could maneuver and despite its mammoth size the moving target would present difficulties for the attackers.

The *Akron* did not have its own planes for use in the exercise, since only one Curtiss *Sparrowhawk* had been delivered. Had she carried her maximum of five scouts, they would have sighted the enemy while using the *Akron* as an airborne carrier with the airship not being sighted at any time. Not having to head into the wind to launch her scouts, the *Akron* had a time advantage over the surface carrier, which had to head into the wind for launching and recovering planes. The airship scouts could be launched into clouds or fog, an impossibility with surface-launched planes.

At 9:09 p.m. June 4 the *Akron* returned from the scouting exercise and was moored at Sunnyvale. Two days later she made a short cruise in the San Francisco Bay region and completed the three hour flight for a party of prominent citizens at 7:06 p.m. A similar flight was made June 9th.

Two days later the weather was right for returning to Lakehurst. The ship was unmoored from Sunnyvale at 10:14 a.m. and the course was set down the Santa Clara valley and through Gilroy Pass to Monterey Bay. By 10:51 a.m. the ships two planes had met the *Akron* and were housed aboard. Passing the coastline by dead reckoning, Rosendahl ordered the ship to be dived through the fog in order to follow the coast southward. The bottom of the fog layer was at 1,000 feet above the surface, and the temperature was 20 degrees cooler than on top of the fog.

At 2:25 p.m., off Santa Barbara, the propeller and hub from No. 3 engine was lost overboard. The prop suddenly went to pieces and splinters tore through the cover, holing the adjacent gas cell. Fortunately, the engine's radiator caught most of the splinters so they did not enter the ship. Part of the transmission shaft had failed.

Sunnyvale didn't have the facilities to make the repair, and Rosendahl decided not to return but to continue on the remaining seven engines to Lake-

hurst. At 4:40 p.m. she was circling the U. S. Fleet at San Pedro. For an hour the airship was accompanied by a squadron of planes from the Naval Reserve Air Station at Long Beach. The *Akron* flew at 3,800 feet to negotiate the high valley land at Banning, California. At 7 p.m. she passed between two 10,000 feet peaks and sighted the Salton Sea. The wind in the pass was 45 knots and extremely hot and dry. The air flowing over the rough topography brought very turbulent air, and full speed was called for on the engines for adequate control. Over the Salton Sea the temperature at 4,000 feet was 94 degrees.

At 8:22 p.m. the *Akron* was over Yuma, and she followed the lighted airways via Phoenix, Tucson, Douglas and on to El Paso, Texas.

Over Phoenix at 4,500 feet at midnight the temperature was 94 degrees. The helium expanded, reducing the height at which the *Akron* could travel. Only 50 miles away the ship would have to be taken to 6,000 feet to get through the narrow mountain passes. To make the required altitude, all ballast and a considerable amount of fuel would have to be jettisoned.

"Pump fuel into the after dump tanks," ordered Rosendahl. "We'll drain them in flight."

The temperature finally dropped to 76 degrees, after 12,400 pounds of fuel had been vented. Since it was still night, the captain held off putting the two planes overboard to save weight. With all seven remaining engines going wide open to sustain the ship's heaviness dynamically due to the loss of helium, she was flown at a five degree angle toward Tucson.

By daybreak they reached Douglas, Arizona. Lts. Harrigan and Young were ordered to take their planes and proceed independently. The airship followed the Rio Grande river to pass south of Van Horn, and the ship cruised through in extremely turbulent air. Three Army planes approached the ship from El Paso at Van Horn and then turned south. The *Akron* followed the railroad to Pecos, but the ship was still heavy and it was impossible to embark the airplanes again. In the trip through the mountains gusts had driven the ship to 6,100 feet and more helium had been lost.

Lt. Ward Harrigan took off in the Curtiss *XF9C* and radioed the *Akron* that the *N2Y* had problems and would have to be dismantled and shipped by freight to Lakehurst. A short time later the *Akron* received a radio report that sand had been dis-

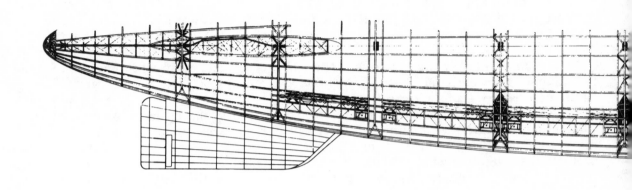

BAY NO.			0			I			II			III			IV		
MAIN FRAMES - STA. NOS.	-23.75					0			17.5			35			57.5			80
INTERMEDIATE FRAMES - STA NOS.	-26.75	-20.50	-16.25	-11.25	-6.25		6.25	11.25		23.75	28.75		41.25	46.25	51.25		63.75	68.75	73.75

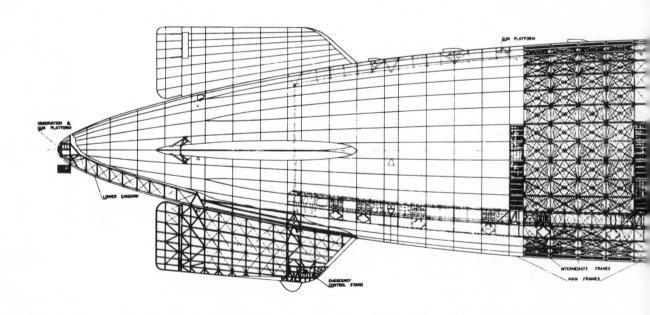

OBSERVATION &
GUN PLATFORM

LOWER GANGWAY

GUN PLATFORM

EMERGENCY
CONTROL STAND

INTERMEDIATE FRAMES

MAIN FRAMES

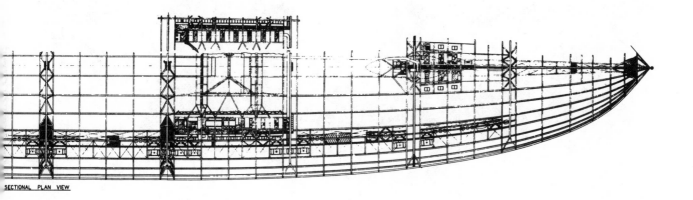

SECTIONAL PLAN VIEW

06.25   102.5   VI   125   VII   VIII   170   IX   187.5   X   198.75   210.75
                108.75   113.75   118.75   131.25   136.25   141.25   147.5   153.75   158.75   163.75   176.25   181.25   183.76   202.75   208   208.5   213.5

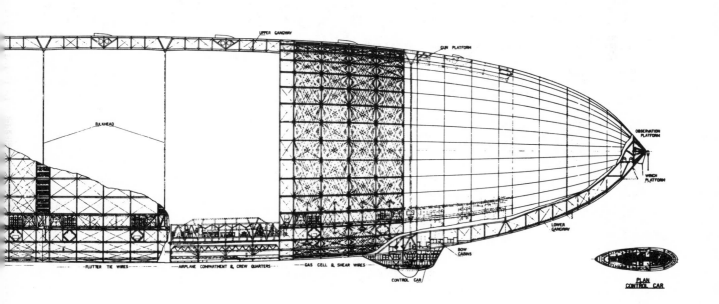

After landing and mooring over drenched terrain, the *Akron* prepares to depart Parris Island, S.C.,
June 14, 1932 on the last leg of her return flight from the west coast. Crewmen board via the control
car while youngsters watch.
Navy Dept photo in The National Archives.

covered in the fuel lines of the *N2Y* and that both planes could now proceed to Lakehurst. It was a long cross-country, complicated by the fact that the airship could not provide the two planes with adequate charts for their guidance.

Flying via Odessa, Midland, Big Springs and Abilene, the airship went over Cleburne, Texas, Rosendahl's home town whence he had gone to the Naval Academy as a plebe 22 years earlier.

Reaching Shreveport at 2 a.m., the *Akron* cruised smoothly eastward, despite a line of thunderstorms to the north and another to the south. She reached Montgomery, Ala. at 10:58 a.m., amid rapidly rising cumulus clouds from thunderstorms which had preceded the ship's arrival. The *Akron* flew between 5,000 and 6,000 feet to stay above the clouds, but as the day progressed these increased in height and the ship had to go below them. Passage was rough for the rest of the day. Depletion of fuel, loss of superheat from the high temperatures and bad weather at Lakehurst made a stop at Parris Island mandatory.

At 4 p.m. the radio operator brought a message to the captain from the mooring officer at Parris Island. The field there was flooded, and the riding-out circle was consequently in bad condition.

Rosendahl consulted with Dresel.

"General thunderstorm conditions are over the entire east coast," the captain said.

"We don't have sufficient fuel to wait for it to clear," Dresel said.

"We'll stick to my earlier decision to land now," Rosendahl said.

At 6:35 p.m., despite a steady rain, the airship was moored at the expeditionary facility. Half the mooring circle was flooded and the ground crew waded in places two feet deep. Much of a cinder path prepared for the stern taxi wheel had washed away. Fortunately, the wind direction made it possible that the ship's stern carriage occupied the "best" part of the cinder path. At 9:25 p.m., however, the wind shifted 100 degrees in a torrential downpour of rain. The ground crew could not keep up with the rapidly swinging stern wheel. Passing a washed out spot, the taxi wheel at the stern struck with a terrific impact. Somehow the wheel was not torn from the ship. Marines, carrying shovels and buckets, filled in the riding-out circle throughout the rainy night. A truck and tractor tried to haul cinders as needed but became hopelessly mired to their hubcaps. They were deep enough so the ship

would swing over them. Finally the cinder path was improved so that the ship could oscillate for the period of the ship's sojourn.

Difficulties in obtaining the proper fuel containing tetraethyl lead for the high compression engines delayed departure, and the airship had to await clearing weather and sunshine to pick-up superheat in order to leave. Six tanks of fuel were pumped back to the mast for storage in order that ballast could be kept aboard to take care of the night's rain load. No helium was available to solve their problem. By 10 a.m. June 15 sufficient superheat had been received. The pelican hook in the release pendant jammed, and for several minutes it appeared the ship had been cast off in some jeopardy. However, it was freed, and after leaving the Marine Base the ship went to 6,000 feet to fly over squall clouds.

When they reached the Maryland coast altitude was decreased to a thousand feet to get under the clouds and take advantage of a favorable southeasterly wind as noted from observing the surface of the ocean. At 5:30 p.m. north of Atlantic City, Rosendahl set the course directly for Lakehurst, meeting very low clouds, fog and rain. The tailwind had given the *Akron* a groundspeed of 82 knots while cruising on her seven good engines at 53 knots.

Ground tackle had been laid out for an approach from south southwest, but as the ship headed in to land, the wind shifted more than 180 degrees. The *Akron* dropped the lines but the winds aloft were still shifting. One of the trail ropes fouled and so both were cast adrift. Suddenly, a dense passing fog set in. The ship circled and made another approach in intermittent fog and was able to complete the mooring without incident at 7:08 p.m. A little over an hour later the ship was housed in a dense fog that had set in for the night.

The West Coast trip was completed. The ship had been away from home base for 38 days—twice the time the *Shenandoah* had spent on her similar pioneering trip eight years earlier.

LCdr. Rosendahl set about advising Admiral Moffett on the need to modernize the mooring system and provide more adequate facilities for such long overland journeys. He pointed out in his report that the proper utilization of airships was overwater and that overland cruises using the primitive expeditionary masts were not in the best interests of airship safety. Briefly, he recom-

Above, in slow flight, Lt. Howard L. Young
ascends to the trapeze of the *Akron* May 3, 1932
in the Curtiss *XF9C-1* Sparrowhawk over water.
This marks the beginning of hook-on plane operation as the airship prepares for the West Coast
flight. At right, another hook-on, over snow-
covered terrain.
Official U.S. Navy photos.

mended (a) provison of mobile yaw guy anchorages, (b) yaw guy equilization, (c) improved mooring winches, and (d) vertical control during the mooring operation.

The mooring operation currently involved three wires: the main mooring wire by which the ship's mooring cone was pulled into the mast cup against the buoyancy of the ship; and two yaw or nose-steadying wires to prevent yawing or lateral displacement as well as preventing the ship from over-riding the mast top. Wind direction changes during mooring required shifting yaw guy anchors. Shift-

ing the yaw guys put the whip in jeopardy just when the steadying influence was most needed. Rosendahl recommended making the yaw guy anchorages—concrete anchorages of snatch blocks laid out at 7½ degree intervals on the circle of 500 feet radius about the mobile mast. The low mast mooring installation with the circular railroad track for the stern car would lend itself well to the project.

On the West Coast trip, *Akron* had made 16 individual flights, totaling 386 hours in flight. She had covered 17,901 statute ground miles.

Over the Empire State Building, Central Park behind her, the *Akron* heads back to Lakehurst after visiting New York.
Official U.S. Navy photo.

One of the six Curtiss *F9C-2's* approaches the trapeze. Normal cruising range for scouting operations was 176 miles at 125 m.p.h. with a maximum speed of 200 m.p.h. with landing gear removed. *Official U.S. Navy photo.*

CHAPTER SEVEN

Happy Days Here Again

As a candidate for the Master of Science degree in Aeronautical Engineering at M.I.T., Lt. (jg) Hammond James Dugan spent the winter of 1931-32 deep in study. The light in the study in Charles Morton's beautiful house in Belmont, Mass. was lit until one, two and three in the morning. Late at night studying was a privilege not permitted at the Naval Academy a decade earlier, and he had not forgotten getting demerits as a young midshipman for burning the midnight oil.

Often he would run wind tunnel tests on his wooden model of the *Akron* until 9 p.m. before coming home to study. In February, he passed the first semester standing high in his class. In eight subjects he passed three with honors, four with credit and he successfully passed the course in airplane design practice—a subject at which a Lighter Than Air man might be expected to have more difficulty than one specializing in Heavier Than Air.

In the few moments he had from his technical work, Dugan kept current through his host Charles Morton on the changing political scene that was changing the life of America.

Franklin Delano Roosevelt was elected President over the colorless yet able Herbert Clark Hoover. The nation, struggling in its worst depression, had voted out the unsmiling, round-faced chief executive who felt he could not institute reforms without broad legislative changes.

Roosevelt, only child of a wealthy aristocratic family, had set out to understand the working man. He had served as Assistant Secretary of the Navy and had been Governor of New York. At the age of 39 he had contracted polio, which left him paralyzed from the waist down. His infectious smile, confidence and positive attitude offered the image of leadership to get the country out of its dilemma. His charming wife, Eleanor, encouraged him to seek the presidency. Now he was set to take the helm of state. Roosevelt's ever-present cigarette in a holder held at an upright angle or clamped in his teeth while smiling, a cocky tilt of his chin, promised optimism and hope in the face of millions unemployed, dust storms and families in shanty towns named "Hoovervilles."

World War 1 veterans, promised a $500 bonus by 1945, marched against Washington and attacked civil servants as they left work to go home. Hoover, in his last days in office, refused to see their leaders. With Gen. Douglas MacArthur in charge, aided by Major Dwight Eisenhower, troops turned back the veteran mob and restored order to Washington.

Roosevelt flew to Chicago to address his nominating convention. He promised a crusade to restore America, and his theme song was "Happy Days Are Here Again."

That March of 1932 Lt. Dugan received his orders from the Bureau of Navigation to report June 7 for duty involving flying aboard the *U.S.S. Akron*, upon completion of his course of training at M.I.T.

As his course neared the finish, the Mortons and Dugans at Belmont exulted in news of the first solo crossing of the North Atlantic in an airplane by a woman, Amelia Earhart Putnam. Her Lockheed Vega had flown from Harbour Grace, Newfoundland to Londonderry, Northern Ireland.

Dugan was polishing up his thesis throughout the Spring of the year. His investigation was to determine the air forces on the *Akron* when moored in the wind at angles between zero and 90 degrees and the distribution of the forces at a

Lt. (jg) Hammond James Dugan
(USNA '24) studying.
Maryland Historical Society photo.

particular angle of yaw. He spent endless hours in the five-foot wind tunnel at M.I.T. In his test set-up, a vertical board represented the ground and was fixed in the tunnel at the mooring distance from the model.

His tests were made both with and without fins on the model to correlate between the forces and pressure measurements. Results, shown on various curves, showed that rather large vertical forces existed, tending to lift the ship off the ground. At the same time, side forces of somewhat greater magnitude than are found in free air exist at the same average speed and yaw. The fins reduced the vertical force somewhat when the model was at the same negative angle of pitch at which the full-sized ship was moored.

Dugan concluded that side forces increased almost linearly with the angle of yaw to about 60 degrees, at which point they flattened out some-what. He found that the present docking and un-docking operations imposed considerably higher aerodynamic loads than those which were imposed by earlier manual methods of mooring. There was a definite tendency of air to flow *around* rather than *over* the obstacle on the ground—the airship—when the atmospheric temperature gradient was below normal.

As Dugan prepared to leave the wind tunnel for the last time, he patted the 1/250th scale wooden model fondly. The model, along with the miniature mobile mast and stern handling beam, would be returned to the David Taylor Model Basin.

His long hours of study paid off handsomely. Dugan was third highest man in a class of 38 at the graduate school. June found him with a master's degree in Aeronautical Engineering, which was not usual for naval officers. While Frances took her new baby boy, Charles Hammond Dugan, to visit with the elder Dugans in the Catonsville section of Baltimore, Lt. Dugan reported to Lakehurst and looked for a house for his new family.

On June 2, Frances received a Western Union wire:

"HAVE HAD ESTIMATE $150 TO MAKE PLACE LIVABLE. DINING, LIVING, SITTING, BED, KITCHEN AND BATH ON FIRST FLOOR. TWO BEDROOMS SECOND FLOOR. RENT $20 GREAT LOCATION AND GROUNDS. NEED A WEEK HERE TO PUT IN SHAPE. RED."

The little house overlooked the lake and was shaded by pine trees and off by itself. When

Frances arrived, with little "Chiefie"—his brown skin and light hair making his eyes bluer than ever— she beamed her approval. Frances graciously refused the offer of Mrs. Dresel, wife of the soon-to-be new captain of the *Akron*, to share their house while the Dugans fixed up the little house. She busied herself buying wallpaper, moving in antiques and turning the house into a delightful home.

Soon, despite the fact that the land was posted, people out strolling would walk through the grounds. On one of their first coffees, a foreign woman stopped and stared.

"'t'is a dream house, 't'is a dream house," she said.

Their dog, Shady, soon to have puppies, wagged her tail in approval.

It didn't take long for the Dugans to feel at home with the intimate LTA family at Lakehurst. By mid-June, the new hook-on plane pilots reported for duty—Fred Kivette, "Swede" Larson and H. B. "Min" Miller. Dugan had been on leave while they were fixing up the house and on the 20th, a few days after the *Akron's* return from the west coast. He was on active duty with the ship as Assistant 1st Lieutenant and Deck Division Officer, under Lt. Roland G. Mayer.

On Wednesday, June 22, at 8 a.m., the crew was mustered in the big hangar by the ship and LCdr. Rosendahl read orders detaching himself from command of the vessel. Cdr. Alger Dresel read orders assigning him to command the *Akron*. Dresel, a veteran of sea duty in China who also had commanded the *Los Angeles*, was popular with the crew. He had shown that he felt airships had their limitations and it was felt he wouldn't take unnecessary chances in adverse weather just to ease the pressure from Washington and the Fleet to make the airships perform.

Toward the end of June the crew and civilian aircraft mechanics were busy making rapairs to the ship. In the economy wave, the *Los Angeles* was decommissioned on June 30. On that date, Cdr. Frank Carey McCord reported for duty under instruction as prospective commanding officer, understudying Dresel.

The four new hook-on pilots began getting plenty of practice. During one landing by Lt. Jeter, the newest pilot to report for duty, the landing hook refused to release the plane. Lt. Roland Mayer, who had come forward in many an

Crewmen inspect gas cells aboard the *Akron*. The airship's dozen cells are made of cotton cloth protected by gelatin-latex. *Official U.S. Navy photo*.

emergency, climbed down the trapeze and pounded on the hook for ten minutes with a hammer. Finally it became free. Mayer climbed into the open cockpit forward of Lt. Jeter in the *N2Y* and they flew down to the air station, repaired the hook and returned. The *N2Y* was hoisted aboard and Mayer was congratulated. It was not the first time the hang-up had occurred. On the *Los Angeles*, Lt. George Calnan had done the same thing. That summer he was leading the atheletes as they took oath at Los Angeles for competing in the Olympics. He was fencing in competition against international fencers for the fourth time. After the event, he was slated for duty aboard the *Akron*.

Frances Dugan, busy caring for her infant son, never tired of seeing the poetic beauty in the big ship that was such a big part of her husband's life. One night an unforgettable sight was the *Akron* flying over the lake, the upper half invisible in the mist. Fog rolled past her sides in long streamers. It gave her a feeling of safety, looking so substantial in the air ocean above her little green-shingled house on the lake.

One night in July "Red" had gone up on the *Akron* for a 24-hour flight so the planes, looking like mosquitoes, could practice hooking-on. The ship looked more beautiful than she had ever seen it. She watched in rapture as the ship flew across the lake and into the moon—literally.

Dresel's schedule was to fly the ship from Monday through Thursday. The visiting public relations director for Goodyear, Hugh Allen, felt the cautious schedule could sink the airship cause. Dresel had turned down a projected trip to Hawaii when everyone from the Commander-in-Chief down were agreeable. Allen felt that Rosendahl was a strong spokesman for the Navy and that Dresel's coming six months in command would not do the airship much good. He became a fast friend of the Dugans and corresponded regularly.

On July 5, the *Akron* was being readied for a flight on which she would search for the missing yacht, "Curlew." Lt. Dugan drove the Ford to the hangar with Frances and their infant boy, "Chiefie." She would take the car back to their home by the lake. There being time to kill while awaiting the signal to take the airship from the hangar, Dugan escorted his wife into the hangar through the tremendous doors.

Entering the inside of the ship through the ladders in the control car, Frances became one of the few women who ever saw the inside of a large Naval airship. The experience was awe inspiring—it reminded her of being inside a cathedral in Milan or Paris or York. Truly, the design of such behemoths was one of the miracles of the Twentieth Century!

With the wind low at sunset, Frances and "Chiefie" watched as the ship was taken out to the mooring circle and then departed about 7,p.m. The trip took the *Akron* to Bermuda, a flight of 2,246 miles all told as they looked in vain for the missing yacht, while at the same time completing operational exercises for the officers and men. The next day, Wednesday they returned. Frances watched her arrival from the Dugan home. It was dusk, and there were many vari-shaped gray and opaque clouds. The *Akron* seemed chameleon-like, having the same color as the clouds, but such a smooth, symmetrical form. Her twinkling lights made her like a fairy ship.

The big ship was in. Her silver shape was partly hidden by the oncoming blackness. Searchlights played on the ship as the *Akron* was held to the movable mooring mast and was readied for the hangar.

Zero hour the next morning was at 4:45 a.m. The Dugans arose at 4:20 a.m. and Frances drove "Red" to the hangar, having left "Chiefie" alone at the house. Cdr. Rosendahl was at the station and she had an opportunity to talk to him at length. She liked him immensely.

"Cdr. Dresel is a wonderful man," Frances told Rosendahl. "The Dresels offered us their home when we were decorating the house by the lake," she added.

"We both think a lot of 'Red', Frances," Rosendahl said. "He is one of the bright stars of the upcoming officers in our little band."

When Frances returned to the house by the lake, she was elated that "Chiefie" was still sleeping. His father was off on the short local flight while the "hook-on" planes practiced.

On Thursday, July 14 the ship made a local flight of 975 miles. On the 20th she flew 1,143 air miles, via Baltimore, Washington, Fredericksburg and Barnegat to the air station. In mid-week, July 26-27, the ship flew 2,276 air miles along the Atlantic Coast. None of the flights was as beautiful to "Red" Dugan as the one to Bermuda, with its green islands and coral reefs.

On Thursday July 28, Lt. Richard F. Cross, Jr., a family man with two children, reported for duty as engineering officer for the *Akron*.

Cdr. Dresel's schedule gave the officers and men of the crew a chance to fly without undue pressure. A coastal flight Aug. 2 covered 1,021 miles. A week later the flight was 841 air miles. August 11, cruising 1,737 miles, she flew over the ocean for hook-on tests. Friday, August 19, it was 629 air miles.

August 22nd marked six months to the day from the costly accident of February 22 under Cdr. Rosendahl's command. This time Dresel was to get the special headache when something went wrong. After supper time the ship was being undocked. LCdr. Herbert Wiley took his station near the stern beam, within six feet of the telephone talker whose phone was relaying signals to the control car. Between Wiley and the mast holding the airship Seaman 1st Class Hurley Ashcroft held the light signal which upon order would be flicked to green to direct moving of the mast once the stern beam was clear. Lt. Robert Sayre had replaced Lt. Roland as mooring officer, and in the ten months of the ship's operation few officers had much experience in manipulation of the mast, which itself had been operable for only six months. Unknown to Sayre, Cdr. Dresel had an understanding with his previous mooring officer, Roland, that the ship would not be moved until word was received from aft over the telephone rather than from the light signal alone.

The stern handling beam had not yet been moved clear of the ship, but Lt. John M. Thornton, working with Wiley and Sayre, believed the beam was clear.

The ship was heading westward, 297 degrees True. Wind was from the south at six knots.

"Give the green signal," ordered Lt. Thornton to Ashcroft. The young sailor obeyed.

"Move the beam toward the hangar," ordered LCdr. Wiley. Lt. (jg) Wilfred Bushnell, on the starboard side of the after control car, noticed the ship was about to hit the beam.

"Stop the beam!" yelled Bushnell. The beam had moved from six to fifteen feet when the stern met the beam and was carried 25 wrenching feet before the beam was stopped. The mobile rail mooring mast to which the ship's bow was attached had been moved facing 297 degee true and the beam was not completely cleared from under the ship's lower fin. The pedestal on the taxi wheel under the after control car collided with a crunch on the stern handling beam.

A truck of the beam lurched off the track of the hauling up circle. Wiley followed the movement and heard a loud noise of breaking girders. He looked unhappily at the newly wrinkled girder metal along the bottom of the lower fin.

When LCdr. Edwin "Bunny" Cochrane, assembly and repair officer, surveyed the damaged, he estimated from $9-11,000 in labor and $2,000 in material.

At the Board of Investigation several days later, Chief Radioman Robert Copeland testified that from his position at the control car switchboard he had received no word that the ship was ready aft. Yet the bow had been moved. The Board came to the conclusion that the lack of experience in having only six months operating the stern beam absolved any of the officers concerned. LCdr. Wiley could not have controlled the premature displaying of the light, since he had not heard Lt. Thornton's order to Seaman Ashcroft. The mishap served to clarify procedures in the difficult ground handling of the ship.

At the end of August, the officers threw a party for Lt. Wilfred Bushnell, who was detached from the ship and put on temporary duty with the Navy Balloon Team. The heavy-set officer was congratulated on his selection to compete and was given a hearty send-off for Basle, Switzerland. Lt. "Tex" Settle, who was in on the festivities, was on leave from the Goodyear-Zeppelin Corporation, where he was supervising inspection of the new airship, ZRS-5. Bushnell and Settle went on to win the Gordon Bennett Balloon Race with a 921-mile flight record.

The flying schedule got heavier in August. After one 72-hour flight from which "Red" Dugan had arrived at dawn, he had to go to bed at 8 p.m. On another flight, the Akron was due to return to the station in the evening but a storm hit the air station. The airship cruised all night. At dawn there was a fog. At the little house by the lake, Frances could hear the drone of the engines above the fog, but she couldn't see the ship. Finally, the fog lifted, and the ship landed. Frances greeted her husband at the hangar.

"Where did you go last night?" she asked, as she hugged him in his fur-lined flying suit.

He took the heavy suit off with tugs and pulls.

"We turned our back on the storm that was chasing us out to sea," Dugan said. "Then we faced it head-on and went right through it. Wasn't very

After the prototype *XF9C-2* was built, Curtiss produced six *F9C-2* hook-on planes in less than a year for the Navy. Each is powered by a 438 h. p. Wright R-975-E3 engine.
Official U.S. Navy photo

exciting—the ship is so large."

That night, a part-time maid, Pat, ironed table linens for several hours, while "Red" read Thackeray's "Vanity Fair" to Frances. The peaceful domestic scene, with "Chiefie" sleeping in his crib, could have represented the quiet, peaceful hours of any family man from a less hazardous occupation.

The month September was relatively uneventful. The summer thunderstorm season ended and the skies became clearer for smooth flying.

The Dugans got to know some of the other couples better. Lt. Scott E. Peck, known as "Scottie," was navigation officer. He and "Red" would discuss the ship and Peck was of the opinion that the handling of the ship at the lower fin station as designed put undesirable strain on that part of the *Akron.*

LCdr. Don Mackey's wife offered comic relief in the well circulated story that she was not overly fond of cooking. The station joke had it that when Don came off a flight, eager for good home cooking his wife would greet him saying:

"Here honey," she pointed to the pantry. "Just pick yourself a little old can."

A gaggle of young lieutenants reported in September: Charles W. Roland, Richard Clendenning, George Calnan—the fencer—and Howard N. Coulter. The Dugans were especially friendly with the Calnans.

Early in the month 26 men, half of them civilians, were busy repairing the lower fin after a hard landing. As the month ended, gas cell no. 2 was removed and laid out for inspection. Several small holes in gas cell no. 3 also were patched. No. 2 cell was scheduled for complete replacement in October.

By October 1932, Maryland banks were closing.

"That $200 we saved for the new baby may just pass from us forever," Frances told her husband.

"With the lady inside and the smile on the face of the tiger," said Dugan.

With Fall, the airship took on different harmony in the color scheme of nature. One afternoon the *Akron* came in over the lake about 4:30 p.m. Frances could see her better by her relection than in the sky. The nose was gold from the sunset, and shaded back to a silvery purple.

"Red" Dugan now had more than a thousand hours in the air. He looked ever so peaceful, puffing on his pipe in their living room and reading Shaw's "An Intelligent Woman's Guide to Socialism."

The autumn of 1932 had seen the economy move hit the military hard. A 15 per cent pay cut put the Dugan salary back to what an officer got in the first decade of the century. As time went on, however, they realized their money in the Baltimore bank was still safe.

Dark-haired and handsome, Harold B. "Min" Miller was a regular dinner guest. One night, he and "Red" studied until 12:30 a.m., with stacks of technical books on the table by them. Frances thought if the public knew of the studying necessary to get ahead in the service, they would be proud of the men who wore the uniform of their country. Bluejackets and Marines were now getting a salary of $17 a month to start. Both officers had received word that they would eventually be on the crew of the new sister ship to the *Akron,* due to be ready in the Spring of 1933. Miller was next in line to the senior hook-on pilot to command the HTA unit on the new airship. Dugan had to "get his number" to make full Lieutenant by June.

The end of October the *Akron* went on a 24-hour flight. It was a rough day and Dugan took the elevators on one watch. He found it an "ungodly workout," but he managed to keep the ship within a few hundred feet of her assigned altitude. He was consoled in the fact that he didn't make anybody sick. His experience at the controls of the *ZMC-2* had made him one of the most skillful of the LTA fliers at Lakehurst.

In November, they made a number of local flights, and on Nov. 22 they took Rear Adm. Moffett on a flight over New York City, which Dugan always enjoyed. Rear Admiral F. H. Schofield of the General Board was aboard, and he flashed a light to the second floor of the Chrysler Building, where his son worked.

"One of my ancestors owned Manhattan Island," Schofield told Dugan, as they looked at the skyscrapers.

"I guess if it weren't for the shipping capability here," Dugan said, "None of the wealth represented below would be here, Admiral."

Dugan, as assistant first lieutenant, started keeping a pocket log in November. His leather bound "Aviator's Flight Log Book" credited Captain Dresel with two flights that month, totaling 35 hours and 53 minutes. December was better, with three flights totaling 59 hours and 27 minutes.

Contact of skyhook and trapeze leaves the
Sparrowhawk subject to the whims of bumpy
air until Lt. Young guides a stabilizing arm into
one of the pair of jaws on the upper wing of the
XF9C-1.
Official U.S. Navy photo.

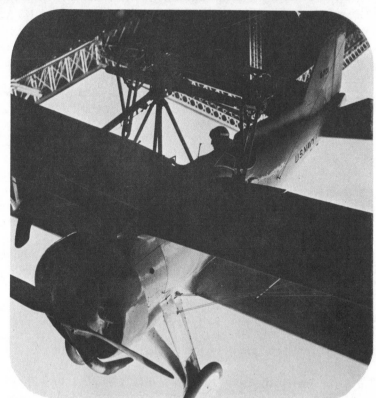

Midway through the *Akron's* hangar door, Lt. Young switches off
the engine of his Sparrowhawk. By
monorail, the Curtiss *XF9C-1*
is transferred to a corner of the
hangar, so that other planes might
be embarked or debarked. Trunk-like
pipe under propeller's center is a
blast tube to bring air to engine's
magnetos.
Official U.S. Navy photo.

On Saturday Dec. 3 the crew was paraded in the hangar for change of command ceremonies. Capt. H. E. Shoemaker was relieved as commanding officer of the station by Cdr. Fred T. Berry.

Two officers were sent to Miami to inspect the mooring mast for a projected trip by the airship early in January. LCdr. H. E. MacLellan reported for duty as navigator on the *Akron*.

"Red" Dugan successfully got through his physical for flying again. While he was taking it, short Lt. Anthony Danis was also taking his exam.

The doctor noted that Danis was an inch shorter than the required height for duty in flying, but made a typographical mistake when indicating Danis' height, saying he was 59′ tall instead of 59″. Danis, a valued aerological officer of considerable experience and acumen, was quickly approved to continue flying. The officer over-riding the medic's disqualification noted that since the papers indicated he was 59′ tall, he more than met the prescribed minimum requirements for service in Lighter-Than-Air.

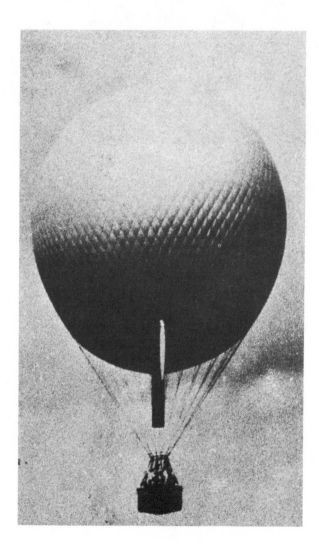

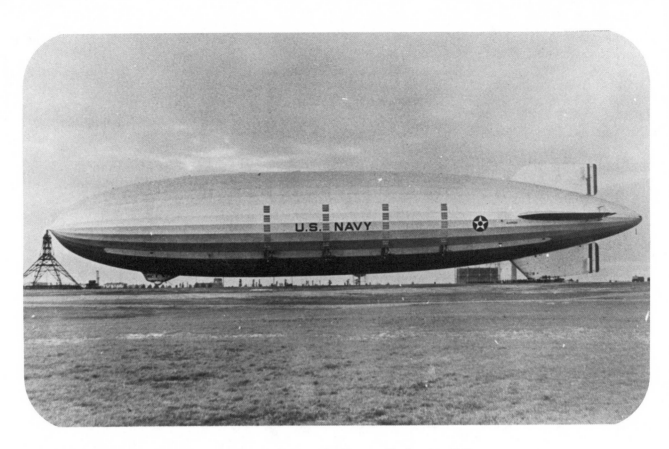

Dwarfing the storage tank and buildings near the mooring mast, the *Akron* readies for take off. She is 785 feet long and 155 feet high.
Official U.S. Navy photo.

CHAPTER EIGHT

McCord Takes Over

The start of a new year in January 1933 brought the *Akron* her third captain in 19 months. Cdr. Frank Carey McCord for the six months previous had been "Makee-Learn" skipper of the airship under Cdr. Alger Dresel.

The first captain, LCdr. Rosendahl, came to command in June 1931 with about 3,500 flying hours experience. He was in command nine months and flew the *Akron* about 800 hours. Dresel became captain in July 1932, with about 1,800 hours' experience, including a year in command of the *Los Angeles*.

Rosendahl had the additional experience of three years in command of the *Los Angeles,* during which he flew her for a thousand hours. Dresel, in his turn, had been captain of that older airship for a year and flew her some 600 hours.

LCdr. Herbert Wiley also had been captain of the *Los Angeles* for a year, and logged the same number of hours as Dresel. Having been executive officer on both airships, Wiley had some 2,000 hours logged as the helm passed on to a new captain as 1933 was launched.

Cdr. Frank McCord had been selected to be captain of the *Akron* after 1,180 hours on the *Los Angeles* and an additional 500 hours on the *Akron* while under instruction. In making the selection of McCord over Wiley, Adm. Moffett and Adm. Upham and their advisers took into consideration that McCord was senior in rank, had superior fitness reports throughout his career and had begun his LTA instruction the summer that the *Shenandoah* went on its final ill-fated flight. With but one airship remaining after that, he had chosen sea duty, serving as navigator aboard the aircraft carrier *Langley* and then to the *Saratoga*. LCdr. Zachary Lansdowne, lost on the *Shenandoah*, had

introduced McCord to Margaret Dodge, whom he married while in his mid-thirties. When his tour of sea duty was over, he became executive officer at Lakehurst, in October 1929.

Now 42 and in the prime of life, McCord's leadership qualities made him the obvious choice to be captain. Wiley had been in the Naval Academy class of 1915, while McCord was graduated in 1911. Despite Wiley's having stayed with the LTA program longer, the Navy did not have reason to bypass the overall experience of McCord in favor of the more specialized experience of Wiley.

Fitness reports for Cdr. McCord began with duty as an ensign aboard a destroyer in 1912-13, when the captain of the *U.S.S. Burrows* reported that McCord was "enthusiastic, conscientious, gets results. Handles men well. Gives promise of becoming an officer of value." Other officers during his three years on that destroyer noted his thoroughness: "uses his head. Not afraid to do a thing and not hesitant. Particularly capable and efficient. Has initiative, judgment and capacity far beyond the average young officer."

A few years later, during World War 1 on another destroyer: 'his ability as engineer officer is outstanding." In 1918, McCord got his own destroyer, the *McComb*. His superior noted that he handled his ship and personnel with marked efficiency. The superlative fitness reports followed McCord as he progressed in his career, including duty up the Yangtse River, where he showed "excellent initiative and has taken care of all American interests in an entirely satisfactory manner."

In 1926-27, while at Lakehurst, Capt. E. S. Jackson rated McCord "calm intelligent, quiet, well-rounded and capable. Even tempered, with

A crewman washes in one of the *Akron's* "heads".
Official U.S. Navy photo.

balanced judgment."

As navigator of first the *Langley* and then the *Saratoga*, McCord kept getting superior reports. When in 1931 he became exec and navigator of the *U.S.S. Los Angeles*, Cdr. Dresel rated him "an excellent officer in every respect. Qualified to command a rigid airship." A year later, on duty on the same airship under Cdr. F. T. Berry, he was again rated as qualified to command a rigid airship.

The turnover of command occurred at 1 p.m. January 3, 1933 and McCord showed immediately that Dresel's leisurely Monday-through-Thursday flight schedule was over. The same day the zero hour for a trip to Miami was set for two hours later.

The actual departure time caught Lt. Hammond J. Dugan by surprise. He hadn't thought he was to be on the Miami flight, and while Frances was out visiting another Navy wife he had to leave a hasty note at the little house by the lake and rush to the big hangar for the zero hour. When Frances returned, she found the Ford gone and a note on the kitchen table:

"Darling: They found they couldn't do without me. The car will be in the hangar if you get someone to drive you up."

While cold weather and dark skies covered the air station, Dugan had a pleasant trip to Miami, with Cdr. McCord guiding his new command over white sandy beaches, glittering hotels and bathers frollicking in the sparkling ocean. On January 5, tied to the expeditionary mast at Opa Locka, the airship rode majestically at her mooring. Dugan, McCord and all the officers were guests of one prestigious country club after another. Miami lionized the airmen, and between golfing, tennis and night clubbing, they thoroughly enjoyed being celebrities of the day. On January 7 the ship left for Guantanamo Bay, Cuba with the two *Sparrowhawks* and the *N2Y* trainer aboard. Their mission was to search for appropriate land on which mooring facilities could be constructed. Lt. Ward Harrigan made a series of ferrying trips to carry a handful of officers down to land and look over the local area. Among them was Cdr. Garland Fulton, who planned to present his recommendations to Admiral Moffett upon returning to Washington after the return flight to Lakehurst and he was back at the Bureau of Aeronautics in Washington.

At the conclusion of the inspection flights to the Cuban areas, Harrigan returned with the front

cockpit filled with lobsters. The general mess enjoyed a Lucullan feast as the airship headed back for Opa Locka, outside of Miami.

Miami again lionized the visiting airshipmen, but when the ship was refueled it was time to recover from all the partying.

As they bade goodbye to Miami's white beaches, Dugan looked down at the beckoning warm waters and could almost feel their coolness, since it was in the upper 80s inside the airship that day. He hoped his share of the officers' mess fund wasn't going to be too hard on the home budget. He was learning that the long trips caused them to stock more food of an epicurean nature, but when the fun was over, each got a bill that had to come out of the household "sock."

Frances Dugan was at the big hangar when the ship came home. She embraced her husband and little "Chiefie" jumped with joy, laughing as he shouted "Daddy! Daddy!" Dugan lifted the youngster up in his arms and held him outstretched as the youngster showed his joy at seeing his father home from his trip to the warmer climate.

In mid-January there were local flights and the last week of the month saw the ship off on an overnight navigation problem. On the return from the 43-hour flight, they had orders to fly over Philadelphia so the citizens could see the ship. The 10-12 knot winds on the surface at Lakehurst began increasing as Cdr. McCord completed the aerial tour of the City of Brotherly Love.

At the Dugan cottage by the lake at the air station, Frances looked forward to her husband's return, but she wasn't sure they would land. The sky became almost black, the wind trying to break the trees in two and waves were pounding on the lake shore.

When the *Akron* reached the station, the gusts were up to 30 knots, making a landing impossible. Cdr. McCord headed the ship north up the Hudson Valley, then west over Lake Ontario and Lake Erie to get behind the storm. Then, from Cleveland he headed east, following the storm as it moved out to sea. The weather finally cleared after a total of 72 hours in flight. The last meal before landing was on the last of the emergency rations: beans, rice, spaghetti, plum pudding and sausages.

Frances Dugan, watching the graceful silver behemoth as it passed low over the lake, noted a big patch on her tail like a corn plaster. Later, at the hangar and the mooring mast area, she saw that

Sky Ships

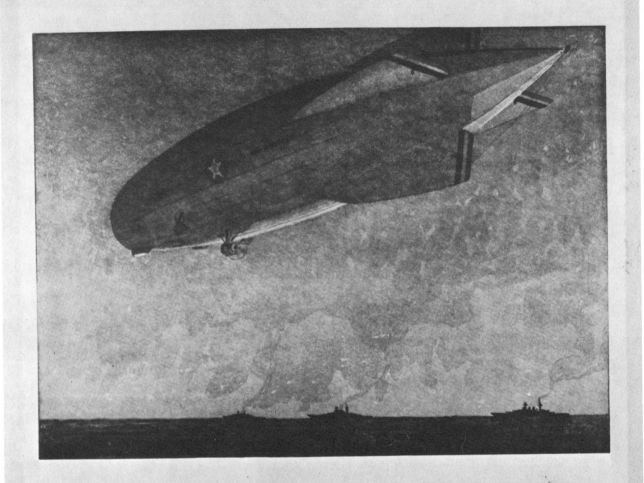

The Navy goes everywhere.

For Broad Experience
JOIN THE U. S. NAVY

it was a collection of snow, accumulated while the ship was following the storm.

When "Red" Dugan finally removed his fur-lined flight suit and relaxed in his little cottage by the pine-fringed lake, he told Frances of the flight as he sipped hot coffee in front of the fireplace.

"That storm just about doubled the time of our flight," Dugan said. "We were in the fog a full twelve hours."

"When did you get on your location?" Frances asked, glowing in the pleasure of having her mate home.

"Bushnell spotted Bellefontaine, Pennsylvania, through a hole in the fog," Dugan said. "Of course, two officers were on the headphones as we went through the soup, guiding the ship on the homing beacons of the commercial airway."

"Weren't you afraid?" Frances asked.

Her husband puffed on his pipe, looking up in surprise.

"No," he said calmly. "Try not to worry about the ship. We have no idea how it can choose its weather, good or bad."

Frances gazed into the fireplace and then back to her husband.

"I saw the big patch of ice on her tail as you came in," she said. "It looked like salt on a giant bird's tail."

"We were carrying tons of ice in the storm but she came through as if the extra load were nothing," Dugan said. "We have complete confidence in McCord. While we were in the fog, firing an echo gun every fifteen minuites to check altitude, McCord didn't leave the control car to sleep for well over twenty-four hours."

Having been out in the *Akron* for 72 hours returning from Miami, Dugan was tired. They turned in early. He was expected to do a full day's work on the morrow. In the evening after work he would work on the stove and the furnace in the cottage, since both needed attention because of his absence.

January saw a total of six flights, totaling 178 hours and 37 minutes—three times what Dresel had logged the previous month.

Lt. Roland G. Mayer was detached from the ship during the month, to report for duty aboard the new sister ship, the *U.S.S. Macon*. No man on the *Akron* was more at home with her 1,500 miles of piano wire, ten million parts and six million rivets. The Construction Corps officer who always came

to the fore in any emergency would be sorely missed. Lt. Anthony Danis and LCdr. "Scotty" Peck also were transferred to the new ship.

During the January flights, the officers recognized a pattern in the leadership of their new captain. McCord seldom asked Wiley, his exec, for advice, and when he did do so, he seldom followed Wiley's recommendations. In an emergency, McCord was decisive. No group discussion among the officers would be made in the control car to arrive at a decision, as had reportedly been done toward the end of the last flight of the *Shenandoah*. On that fateful September 3, 1925, the pioneering Captain Lansdowne reportedly discussed with the others as to whether they should head southeast or south to outrun a storm that was preventing them from going westward. McCord was not one to avoid the initiative, mindful of that situation eight years earlier as published in the official investigation report of the loss of that ship.

Wiley, an efficient officer who had been left a widower with three children when he lost his wife a year before, calmly performed his duties as exec. His LTA experience also had gone back to the days of the *Shenandoah*. During her last flight his assignment was to be at the Detroit mast for the ship's arrival. In subsequent years, he had understudied Rosendahl, Dresel and now McCord. It was an awkward situation—the man of more specialized experience yet junior in rank having to get along with a captain who rated the command because of more senior grade. The two men spoke only on duty matters related to flying the ship. McCord had been countermanded on LTA matters on several occasions while he was exec of the station several years before.

One case in point happened when McCord approved a plan by Lt. "Heinie" Zimmerman, mooring officer, for manually mooring the *Graf Zeppelin*. LCdr. Rosendahl asked to see the plan. Zimmerman provided it and "Rosie" said he instead wanted to see the new mechanical gear tried out. Zimmerman pointed out that the manual plan had been approved already. Rosendahl went to Cdr. Maury Pierce, the station commanding officer and McCord's boss, who directed Zimmerman to make the change that "Rosie" wanted.

Whereas McCord was technically a second generation airshipman, having qualified in free balloons and blimps in 1925, by going to sea after the loss of the *Shenandoah* he missed the continuity

The *Akron* heads east for Lakehurst over Maryland's Eastern Shore.
National Archives photo.

the other officers had and was not third generation. The switch on Zimmerman's mooring plan was just one of a number of occasions when McCord felt as he got started back in LTA that Rosendahl and Wiley—who also was in the picture in the background—had taken advantage of any handicap McCord might have by virtue of his sabbatical at sea.

While McCord was serving as exec of the air station, Wiley was exec officer of the *Los Angeles*, in which capacity he served for three years. With McCord getting his feet wet as exec newly returned from sea duty, Wiley was given command of the *Los Angeles* and set about flying her for another year. Two years after Wiley had come and gone with his airship command—on June 4, 1931—McCord was promoted to Commander. Two months afterwards, he was at last exec of the *Los Angeles* and went on to fly 580 hours understudying Cdr. Alger Dresel, which he logged in addition to some 600 hours under instruction before becoming exec.

With the availability of the new *Akron*, the *Los Angeles* was laid up after eight years of service, and McCord therefore never got the command that had been Wiley's, but went on instead to learn to command the *Akron*. As his flying hours mounted in the big rigids, it became evident he could no longer be looked upon as a "Johnny Come Lately."

On Saturday, January 28 the McCords invited the Dugans to their home for some "cheer," along with the other key airship officers. Peg McCord was a genial hostess and particularly close to Frances Dugan, her contemporary. Frances, a Junior Leaguer, Phi Beta Kappa, horsewoman and on the rifle team in college days, was a lovely woman and a keen conversationalist on a wide range of subjects. "Red" Dugan was up on the latest literary achievements, and together they were a sought-after couple. Frances' uncle had a high position in the government transportation regulatory body, and Peg McCord was a native Washingtonian. McCord himself had graduated from the Naval Academy at age 20, and more than held his own at social gatherings with his well-rounded knowledge.

Included among the small talk at the party was the fact that Japan was giving signs of withdrawing from the League of Nations. Columnists were predicting that Adolph Hitler would be named

Chancellor of Germany by the end of the month. The climate abroad did not look good for continued peace, according to the consensus of military men present.

The rest and relaxation of the weekend came to a close and the following Tuesday the *Akron* was unhoused at 4:40 p.m. and unmoored at 5:35 p.m. with 81 persons aboard. A night navigation problem over sea was begun immediately. At 8 p.m. the ship commenced deceleration tests to obtain data on the ship's aerodynamic qualities. At 9:42 a.m. the *Akron* began calibrating the Bethany Beach, Delaware Radio Compass Station, completing the exercise at 12:40 p.m. Wednesday, February 1. The weather was worsening, with poor visibility and rain.

By 1:15 p.m. Captain McCord and the *Akron* kept her schedule and began calibrating the Cape Henlopen Radio Compass Station. Three hours and a quarter later, the station, noting that conditions were not improving, recommended that the calibration be discontinued. McCord acquiesced. He then ordered the ship to cruise along the Virginia coast in the fog and rain. By 3:30 a.m. the surface was totally hidden by the fog, but the ship cruised over lightships and lighthouses, picking up their fog signals until 7 a.m., when an expected lightship signal was not heard.

Throughout the fog situation it was difficult to judge the exact strength and direction of the wind, since they could not see the ocean. As a result, despite clearing weather at 11 a.m., the expected landfall at Barnegat Light was missed by about eight miles. Near Lakehurst the *N2Y* landed an officer passenger aboard and then returned to the air station. The three Sparrowhawks then conducted rough air tests of the auxiliary trapeze and were hoisted into the ship.

McCord brought the ship in for a landing at 5:47 p.m. Thursday, February 2. An hour and three minutes later she was housed safely in the gigantic Number 1 Hangar.

The next flight, scheduled for the following Tuesday, was postponed because a widespread blizzard was expected to arrive the next day, February 8. Because of the adverse weather, Naval Operations in Washington gave permission to commence overhauling the ship. During the remainder of February, a new Mark IV water recovery apparatus was installed on No. 5 engine, numerous repairs were made on engine auxiliaries,

The *Akron* over Washington, D. C., flying with the *Los Angeles* behind her. Mounds atop the airship are for releasing helium when necessary, done sparingly because of the lifting gas' high cost. *National Archives photo.*

two metal props were installed and several gas cells were partially deflated for inspection and the main frame bulkheads were overhauled.

The last day of the month the scheduled flight had to be posponed because of gales caused by a stationary cyclonic storm off the coast. The strong winds had occurred since February 25, and on the last two days of February the velocity at flying levels was from 60 to 70 knots, with gusts to 70 knots on the surface.

Due to the winter weather, there was only the one flight in February, with a duration of 48 hours 14 minutes. Because of gales at Lakehurst, the flight scheduled for the last day of that month was postponed to the following morning, March 1. The *Akron* left the hangar at 6:30 a.m. and was unmoored at 7:35 a.m. with 96 persons aboard. Among them were two physicists from the Naval Research Lab and a representative of the company that made the new steel propellers. The physicists busied themselves as soon as the ship was airborne testing their sonic drift meter, while the ship was flown at low altitude over water and land for the test.

At 10 a.m. that Wednesday morning a section of fighting planes was received aboard. The three Sparrowhawks were stowed in a quarter-hour elapsed time. Launching took a few seconds longer, since the method involved starting the propellers while the plane was outside the hangar and on the trapeze. The operation was then repeated, with some improvement in the elapsed time. After the hook-ons off Barnegat Light were completed, the *N2Y* was landed ashore.

During the afternoon the ship encountered several snow squalls. When the ship passed over Lakehurst the landing was delayed due to passing snow squalls, but it was completed at 6:19 p.m. in gusty winds up to 30 miles an hour. After riding at the mast a few minutes, the ship was docked in a maximum wind of 17 miles an hour. Newly installed strain gauges in the stern handling lines were used to furnish data on the forces required to dock the ship in gusty winds. On the trip new gust meters installed on the bow by Goodyear Zeppelin Corp. were tested for the first time, but with undetermined results. The metal props installed on engines no. 2 and 3 also were tested.

For a scheduled appearance at the Inaguration Parade for the new president, Franklin D. Roosevelt, the *Akron* was undocked in a strong and gusty

northwest wind at 6:35 p.m. on March 3 and unmoored at 7:41 p.m. with 84 persons aboard. The *N2Y* trainer was received and stowed aboard. The ship's course led southward along the coast to the latitude of Annapolis, at which point the ship headed westward and passed over "Crab Town" and the Naval Academy at 6:45 a.m. March 4. In order not to upstage the Washington festivities, the *Akron* remained in the Chesapeake Bay vicinity until the afternoon.

Over the Eastern Shore, "Red" Dugan received a ride in the *N2Y* biplane while it exercised at hooking on the main and auxiliary trapezes for about an hour. Despite the cold wind on his cheeks, Dugan exulted in the sensation of being in the plane as it approached a stall just before hanging to the trapeze on each successful landing. When it was over, he was glad nothing malfunctioned or jammed, because it was a too wintry to be out in an open cockpit for any long period of time.

The ship approached the Nation's Capitol shortly before 3 p.m., accompanied by several snow squalls, Down below, on Pennsylvania Avenue, Franklin Roosevelt smiled confidently at the crowds. His wife, Eleanor, and son, James, stood by the charismatic new president throughout the five hour inaugural. Roosevelt's leg braces were respected by the news media cameras and few Americans gave a second thought to the physical burden their new President had to bear. Around the nation thousands of banks were closing, but FDR gave heart-warming leadership vibrations to the public as he stood unshivering amid the snowfall.

Aboard the airship, Captain McCord followed the progress of the ceremonies over the broadcast receiver. The airplanes cleared the area and at 3:15 p.m. the airship passed over the Capitol and followed Pennsylvania Avenue to the White House. the *Akron* made two circles to repeat the passage and at 3:57 p.m. departed for Lakehurst, encountering intermittent snow squalls. Arriving at the air station in squally weather, the ship was moored at 7:45 p.m., despite gusts up to 30 miles an hour. The *Akron* rode at the mooring circle until 9:55 p.m., when wind conditions lowered. The vessel was docked at 10:52 p.m., with a maximum wind of 18 miles an hour.

The winter weather was wreaking havoc with the busy schedule that Captain McCord had planned for the ship. He was planning to fly again to Miami

Coming in to the mast. *Akron* is distinguishable from her sister ship by the protuberant gas valves atop the airship.
Official U.S. Navy photo.

March 8, but a period of gales hit Lakehurst which made undocking impossible. Winds of up to 60 and 70 knots velocity were recorded at the station through the 10th, and the first opportunity to undock was early on March 11. The temperature was only ten degrees Farenheit when the ship was unhoused at 2:49 a.m., the operation slowed somewhat due to frozen oil in the locomotive towing the beam on the riding-out circle. The ship did not take off until 4:05 a.m.—another "wee-hours" zero hour, and a Saturday at that.

They had hoped to leave Friday, and Frances Dugan rushed dinner that day at 4:30 p.m. so "Red" could go up to the station. He stayed there until the wind died down and busied himself with the projected pre-dawn departure.

Frances watched the ship with its different colored lights and its nose a luscious silver in the pale light of the full moon. The moon made the night as bright as day. Two tiny planes circled around the airship, like flying ants around a slow-moving cocoon. While families stayed behind, the men of the *Akron* would again enjoy the warmer clime, going on to Panama so sites for mooring stations could be selected.

The *Akron* headed for Cape Hatteras. The weather began improving in the vicinity of Cape Henry and Hatteras was passed at 9:45 a.m. and by 7:45 p.m. the ship reached Palm Beach, Florida. The training plane carying the mooring officer and its pilot departed for Miami and the ship hovered in the vicinity while arrangements were made for landing.

"Red" Dugan took time to write a letter to his wife at 9 p.m., telling her that the moonlight was "perfectly gorgeous." He described passing a hotel every few miles with "brilliantly lighted swimming pools." The temperature at 1,500 feet was 66 degrees, which he quickly calculated would make it about 71 on the ground. Then the signal for landing stations sounded and he broke off the letter to take-up his duties again. The mooring was completed at 9:59 p.m. in a routine manner.

McCord knew that since it was Saturday all the local business firms were closed. They wouldn't be able to obtain the provisions necessary for the Panama flight in time to depart Monday morning.

Over the weekend the airshipmen were again warmly received by Miamians. "Red" Dugan and the officers joined Captain McCord in visits to the Miami Country Club, The Bath Club, the Rod & Reel Club and other exclusive organizations.

By Monday fuel and provisions were received and the heavy winter flight clothing was disembarked for the Panama flight. The *Akron* unmoored from the expeditionary mast at 10:02 a.m. Tuesday March 14, took two airplanes on board in the air and then set a course southwest to cross Cuba in longitude 78 degrees 30 minutes. "Red" Dugan had time to take up his letter to Frances again, and described the flight as "just loafing along above the green Carribbean, flying over lovely blue and green coral reefs with the water unbelieveably clear. Then the Grand Cayman island, with long white beaches lining the clear jade ocean, and green happy towns."

No navigation or land aids were sighted until the next morning, when the breakwater at Colon, Canal Zone came into view.

During the night several mild rain squalls were encountered or detoured. As they reached the breakwater, the ship entered a heavy rainstorm but it dissipated quickly. The ship would remain in the air, of course, since the mission was to look over the location for future installation of a terminal. Five officers were in turn ferried to the Fleet Air Base at Coco Solo to pinpoint a site for an airship terminal. The inspecting party was returned to the ship between 3:48 p.m. and 4:45 p.m. and a few minuites later the *Akron* departed for Isle of Pines, heading north for Florida. On the way they dumped the septic tanks, which weren't made sufficiently large for long cruises in warm weather. The trade winds made progress slow, and they didn't reach Grand Cayman until 10:45 a.m. March 16. On the return trip, only half of the engines were used at one time to conserve fuel. About 2:30 p.m. the *Akron* circled around the east side of the Isle of Pines and approached the southern coast of Cuba with the intention of crossing from Batabano to Havana. Leaving Batabano, a thunderstorm boiled up in the vicinity of Havana and Captain McCord changed course to the west. The storm soon dissipated and the ship arrived there at sunset. To "Red" Dugan, as he looked down on the Morro Castle and Havana, it was one of the loveliest cities he had ever seen. Wide boulevards, lovely gardens, the bay, the harbor, the lights and sunset.

In the city, the ubiquitous shoeshine boys and hustling petty traders gazed at the huge silver ship from street corners, surrounded by garish Coca-Cola signs. Idle young men stopped laughing,

Rear Admiral William Moffett (center) with his sons, George (right) and William, both junior officers. *National Archives photo.*

joking and fighting on the streets to stare at the slow-moving sky ship. The great Caribbean metropolis and its almost two million people were awed by the massive argosy above.

The ship headed for Key West, Fla., and reached the city at 10:30 p.m., continuing thence to Tampa, where the ship cruised on various courses until sunrise. At breakfast "Red" Dugan and his fellow officers looked down on St. Petersburg and then at 8:35 a.m. on Tampa Bay, when the *Akron* exchanged visual calls with the British ship, *H.M.S. Dragon*. Captain McCord then ordered the course changed to the east for Orlando. Reaching the coast, several squalls were in the flight path and McCord deftly detoured around the "red lights" of the sky. Near Palm Beach, the *N2Y* was sent with the Mooring Officer to Miami, and at 7:07 p.m. the mooring was completed, ending the long flight of 81 hours and five minutes.

A week before, when they arrived in Miami, "Red" Dugan had heard the new President's first "Fireside Chat" over the radio. Now he and the other officers and crew had another Sunday free in Miami. Lt. George Calnan's wife had taken the train to the city; so Dugan and the others didn't see much of the tall Olympic fencer during the short stay. On Monday, March 20, President Roosevelt in an economy move signed the Peace Time Navy Act, reducing the pensions of families whose aviators were killed in the Service to only $22 a month for the widow, plus $8 a month for children and $4 for babies. The news wasn't a big item to metropolitan editors and most men of the *Akron* were unaware of the bill and its possible implications. That day, the ship made a local flight and the crew was exercised in camera gun drill, using her planes as targets while flying along the coast. The drill was repeated in the afternoon and the ship then moored at 6:44 p.m., using new yaw winches which had been installed at Opa Locka.

The next day the base was undergoing its annual inspection and the *Akron* rode at the mast rather than request that personnel assist in the ground crew for a departure. Wednesday saw another local flight with camera gun drill, McCord keeping the ship in flight from 8:25 a.m. until mooring at 6:05 p.m., again using the new yaw winches.

McCord had planned to depart for Lakehurst Wednesday March 23rd, but a rapidly moving storm area in south Missouri that was heading eastward caused him to postpone leaving. Instead, a carload of helium was received and the ship was refueled. At 11:16 p.m. that night the ship unmoored; took the planes aboard and headed northward.

The flight proceeded without incident until in the vicinity of Cape Hatteras, where the influence of the rapidly moving storm, now in Virginia, was felt in the form of heavy winds and squally weather. By the time they reached Ocean City, Md., the winds became light and the temperature dropped from 60 degrees to 30 degrees. "Red" Dugan and his suntanned associates quickly donned winter flight clothing. When they reached Atlantic City, low clouds and severe snow squalls were met and visibility was very poor at times. In a light snow fall, the ship was moored at Lakehurst at 4:52 p.m. Frances Dugan and little "Chiefie" were there to meet the head of the family. While waiting for "Red" to be free of his shipboard duties, Frances chatted with Gar Wood, the famous speedboat racer. He was trying out a new camera, on which he had obtained a patent, with the Navy's permission. Hugh Allen, the public relations director from Goodyear Zeppelin Corporation, also was there and talked with them.

Allen was keenly interested in Gar Wood's invention, which provided automatic control of the shutter. As they discussed the camera, Allen remarked that he thought the camera would have wide acceptance in publicity work. Then he waxed philosophical about the giant ship being hauled into the hangar with large clumps of snow still on its tail.

"I have sometimes stood in the dusk at Akron or here and wondered that men have such courage," Allen said. "The ship seems so big and so tall. Almost as though challenging God, daring to take on the rest of creation. But the answer seems to be to take them out and fly them, see what happens, and hope no mistakes are made."

Frances replied: "It has such an air of majesty and a look of safety. 'Red' has complete faith in the ship."

At that point, Dugan left the ship, the last man off. "Chiefie" squiggled and danced until his father picked him up as he always did when returning from a cruise. Gar Wood, after a quick greeting, went off to discuss his camera with other officers at the station. The happy Dugans got into their Ford and went to a warm fireside at their cottage by the lake.

A photo of the *Akron* autographed by her officers. Note four rows of water condensers running up the airship's sides vertically.
Official U.S. Navy photo.

The following Tuesday night, March 28, the *Akron* unmoored at 7:37 p.m. with 78 persons aboard, including Admiral Moffett. The undocking was done in a fresh northwest wind with gusts to 27 knots. Soon after departure, the two fighting planes were received aboard and disembarked for drill. The ship went on to New York and during the night carried out a navigation problem at sea. A feature of the morning radio press was a page of news copied directly from Melbourne, Australia. The big news was that Japan had withdrawn from the League of Nations, following the League's decision not to recognize the puppet state of Manchukuo set up by the Japs early in 1932.

As was standard practice, Captain McCord had sent Adm. Moffett a schedule covering April. On the New York flight, Moffett advised McCord that a letter was coming explaining that only the first half of the April schedule was approved.

"Send me a more detailed outline of programs to be carried out on the various flights, Frank," Moffett told McCord while the two were in the control car. "Airships should operate with specific objectives in view—scouting problems, projecting doctrine for using the airplanes, perfecting internal organization through general quarters and other drills, and so forth."

"Aye, aye, sir," McCord said. This was a new requirement, since such schedules usually were general in nature in the past. The pressure was on to cite specific objectives for each flight. "I'll rework the schedule and get it off to Washington promptly, sir."

The Admiral enjoyed the New York flight and returned to Washington, indicating he might come down for the next scheduled flight within a few days to calibrate the radio station at Newport.

While Dugan, McCord and the other men of the *Akron* enjoyed a Sunday at home, the *Akron* was moored to spring balance scales at the south side of Hangar No. 1, bow to the west. She was approximately two thousand pounds heavy, carried 73,500 pounds of fuel, 1,600 pounds of oil, 28,000 pounds of water ballast and her gas cells were 92 per cent full. Monday evening she would fly again.

Another view of the rudder man's position, taken in the hangar.
National Archives photo.

CHAPTER NINE

Five Hours

Lakehurst Naval Air Station began a new work week as Monday, April 3rd started a new month. The rest and relaxation of the weekend were thrust aside and all hands set about planning the upcoming flight of the *Akron*. Her mission was to calibrate radio direction finder stations of the First Naval District, sending signals while circling the Newport, Rhode Island station commencing at 7 a.m. April 4.

About 11 a.m. Monday Cdr. Frank McCord and his exec, LCdr. Herbert Wiley were in the former's office in connection with flight preparations. The telephone rang and the sailor answering looked at McCord:

"Admiral Moffett would like to talk to you, sir."

McCord, alert and clean-cut, looked at Wiley before taking the 'phone. "Better check the weather while we've got him on the line." Turning to the sailor, McCord said:

"Put the admiral through." He picked up the 'phone and soon he was telling the Bureau of Aeronautics chief of the upcoming flight's outlook. Wylie was phoning for the weather.

"We expect to take the ship from the hangar at sunset, Admiral," McCord said.

Wiley scribbled a brief item as he conversed with Lt. Herb Wescoat. Then he passed the note to McCord.

The captain continued his conversation with the Admiral.

"I've just heard that visibility may not be good enough around Newport tomorrow morning. We can carry out other missions while awaiting clearing, of course."

As McCord listened to the unseen voice on the other end of the line, Wiley and the others stood by. Then McCord said goodbye with a final, "Aye,

aye, sir," and got up from the desk, putting on his blue service cap with gold scrambled egg design on the visor.

"The Admiral's coming along," McCord said cryptically. "Let's go see the morning weather map."

When they reached the aerological office, they found Lt. Wescoat's long face and spaniel-like eyes poring over the 11:30 weather map. He was writing the last bits of information on the map, marking low- and high pressure areas. The leading aerologist on the station, he was known to forecast correctly about 83 per cent of the time—a high rate of reliability. Wescoat would be making the flight with them that night, and he was interested in prognosticating as correct a forecast as possible.

"Right now it appears there will be light winds at sunset," Wescoat told them. He looked at Wiley. "What I told you over the 'phone still holds, however. The fog along the coast will extend inland in the night and will continue in the area of Newport until noon Tuesday."

"Thank you, Lieutenant," said McCord. He and the others left. As they went out the door, McCord ordered Wiley to set the zero hour for 6 p.m.

"Be ready to practice airplane hook-ons in the vicinity of the base," McCord ordered Wiley. "We'll start soon after take-off. After the exercise, embark a training plane."

McCord and Wiley did not meet again until 4:20 p.m., when they again went to the weather shack to view a partial weather map drawn from airways reports received at 4 p.m.

"Visibility will be poor at sunset," McCord told Wiley. "Cancel the hook-ons. We may still be able to take a training plane on board."

All was in readiness for flight. McCord and Wiley went to their homes, the former to give a goodbye

A monoplane's view of the *Akron* and a hook-on plane in flight not far from the big Hangar Number 1 at Lakehurst, New Jersey.
Official U.S. Navy photo.

kiss to his wife of seven years and Wiley to see that his three children would be tended properly by his housekeeper.

The younger officers were at home getting ready for the zero hour. Lt. George Calnan, his sharp, thin face showing that he didn't look forward to leaving Lillian, embraced his expectant wife, saying:

"I feel less reluctant about leaving you now, since I'm leaving something of myself with you."

His pretty wife, who had gone to Miami during the recent flight and spent his shore leave with him then, and had been filled with pride watching him lead the Olympic atheletes at Los Angeles that summer, lingered in his embrace. Then she summoned a stiff upper lip and showed him she had confidence in the safety of the ship, dining with happy talk over a well-cooked meal that she had prepared.

Cdr. "Bunny" Corchrane had called in that he could not make the flight as scheduled. He was down with the flu. His being unable to go made it possible to put a junior officer aboard in his place.

At the Dugan cottage by the lake, the couple had just opened a crate containing an attractive small table and chair, a gift for little "Chiefie's" second birthday. As they admired the new addition to the nursery from the front stoop, surrounded by wisteria and lavender blossoms, Dugan was talking about the new baby, due in July. She had bought Jim workshop tools and he was making plans to build a toy bench to match the new table and chair.

"Did I tell you there is a zero hour at six tonight?" he asked, as an afterthought.

"We'll eat at 5:30, then," Frances answered. "I've planned an amazing salad."

The meal was a gay one. Then a friend's car arrived and Jim Dugan went off to the big hangar. She found herself gazing at a green larch tree and wondering that it was getting darker than normally before a sunset.

She was delayed in getting to see the ship off, and when she reached the landing field she was surprised that fog was about a hundred feet above the ground. Lights playing on the ship went out and the ship's lights took over.

"Up Ship!" was the command. Frances thought the ship looked vital and powerful. As the *Akron* ascended, the encompassing mist took possession, at first with uncertainty and then forcefully. The fog swallowed up the mammoth silver argosy.

As Frances Dugan got back into their Model A Ford and drove home under worsening skies, Lt. Ward Harrigan and the handful of hook-on pilots made certain their Sparrowhawks and the *N2Y* were tied down for the night. The ebullient Harrigan, who had made 350 landings on the ship, was disappointed that the hook-on exercise was postponed. Lt. Fred Trapnell had been ready to go up first to meet the ship. He had to agree with Harrigan that it would be foolhardy to fly up to it through a thousand feet of fog. Both felt McCord's decision was a sound one, and they looked forward to clearing the next noon that would put the scouting airplanes in operation again with the mother ship around Newport.

Aboard the *Akron*, as she ascended through the fog, Lt. Dugan busied himself in the bowels of the ship as engineering officer. In his tan pocket "Aviator's Flight Log" he already had entered the time of departure as 7:28 p.m. and that the outside temperature was 41 degrees Farenheit, the barometer 29.72. The ship, which was to be out 48 hours, carried 73,600 pounds of fuel—enough for five days if necessary. From Dugan's pocket log the data would be taken to fill the large official log pages which were sent monthly to the Director of Ship Movements.

Cdr. McCord ordered a course for Philadelphia, some 35-40 minuites from the station. Reports indicated the ground was visible there, whereas overwater the fog cut visibility of the surface and made it impossible to follow the direction of surface winds.

Rear Admiral Moffett and another half-dozen passengers toured the airship and kept out of the way of the working crew. The Admiral had brought along Lt. Col. A. F. Masury, of the Army Ordnance Reserve, a contractor whose company provided service in the airship program; Cdr. Fred Berry, commanding officer of Lakehurst; and Cdr. Cecil Barton, of the Bureau of Aeronautics. The other three passengers were student officers who needed the time in a large rigid to complete their training: Lt. (jg) Charles Callaway, Lt. Bob Sayre and Lt. Joe Severyns. Sayre had gone aboard when Cdr. E. F. "Bunny" Cochrane had come down with his bad cold.

Over Philadelphia the visibility was fairly good about 8:10 p.m. Cdr. McCord had seen from the earlier forecast that a low pressure area existed westward toward Harrisburg. He planned to run eastward now, since the 8 p.m. weather report was

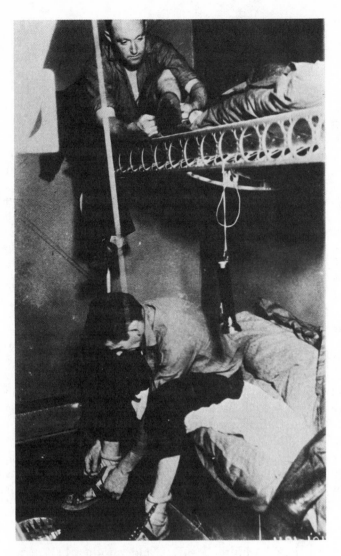

Akron crewmen prepare to go on watch
from their bunks. Tennis-type shoes provide
sure footing while making their rounds of the
airship interior.
Official U.S. Navy photo.

coming in and indicated that a thunderstorm was
now in Washington, D.C. and could be expected to
head rapidly northeastward. By flying east, and
then southeast, the *Akron* would get over the cold
coastal waters and keep ahead of the thunderstorms. The bad weather could pass northward and
then the ship could come around in back of the
last of the bad weather to Newport in time for the
direction finder station calibration.

Lt. Jim Dugan and most of the crew were not
concerned with the flight path of the airship as the
ship killed time in the Delaware River area. Dugan
was busy checking her inner workings. Earlier in
the day, when taking purity readings of the gas
cells, he had noted that cell no. 9 was only 87 per
cent full—indicating the probability of a leak. With
Boatswain's Mate 2nd Class Richard E. "Lucky"
Deal he had located a three-inch tear, caused by
the lower part of the cell getting pinched between
the wires. Finding the leak entailed guessing where
the leak could be by examining any touching wires,
a difficult job with the cell larger than most free
balloons. The two of them patched the leak, thankful that they had found it without too much
searching. In some cases, men were sent tightrope-
walking the cross wires and singing out as they
went along. When the leaking helium caused the
searcher's voice to rise in a falsetto, the leak had
been located. Now Dugan was covering his 785
foot-long "beat" and making entries in his pocket
flight notebook.

"Lucky" Deal was a happy-go-lucky veteran of
14 years in LTA. He was one of the most experienced men in the lower ratings. While on watch in
his section he had chatted briefly with Admiral
Moffett, whom he had known since both had
flown aboard the "*Shenandoah*" in the 1920s. The
Admiral remarked, as he had many times to any
listener, how much he enjoyed his flights aboard a
big rigid airship, no matter what the weather.

While they headed down the Delaware, LCdr.
Wiley left the control car and went into the gun
room in the after part of the car to smoke a
cigarette. The burly exec with the iron-gray hair
had relaxed in the smoking room about twenty
minutes when he felt the engines speed up. Sensing
that something might be awry, he went to the
control car and found that all engines were being
used, running standard speed. The course was now
to the east.

Wiley looked out the starboard window to the

south. There was lightning piercing the black night 25 miles away.

"Maybe we had better run westward," Wiley suggested to McCord.

"I just saw two flashes of lightning to the west," the captain replied.

The two of them watched the lightning. Several times McCord changed the course to the northeast and then back to east, conning the rudder man to go to the left as a reaction to strong lightning flashes getting closer.

"Fifteen degrees to the left," McCord ordered at one point.

"Aye, aye, sir," said the helmsman.

Twenty minutes later McCord checked the compass and found the rudder man had misunderstood him and changed the course fifty degrees instead of fifteen. No harm was done, since the change took the ship still farther from the lightning.

Passing over land now, the ground was soon obscured by fog, but occasionally lights broke through.

"Take her down five hundred feet," McCord ordered. They had been flying at 2,000 feet. "Lucky" Deal was now at the elevator wheel, on the 9-10 p.m. trick. He twirled the wheel. Soon 1,500 feet was the indicated altitude.

The aneroid barometer had been 29.72 when they left Lakehurst. Now the barometer was falling—when it fell to 29.40, the drop would mean an altimeter reading of 1,600 feet would reflect a real height above the surface of 1,280 feet. The setting was never changed in flight. The airmen simply make allowances for the change as indicated by the changes of hundreths of an inch.

About 9:45 p.m. in the vicinity of the coast near Asbury Park the fog layer below had risen to the *Akron's* flying altitude.

"Take her up a hundred feet," McCord ordered. "Lucky" Deal moved the elevator wheel skillfully. The ship levelled off at 1,600 feet indicated altitude, plowing alternately in the clear and then through fog patches.

As they left the coast line, lightning became general and increasingly closer. Soon it was all around and over the ship.

Chief Radioman Robert Copeland hauled in the radio antennae to guard against lightning strikes.

Wiley peered out the open windows, looking upward for thunderheads. He found instead the

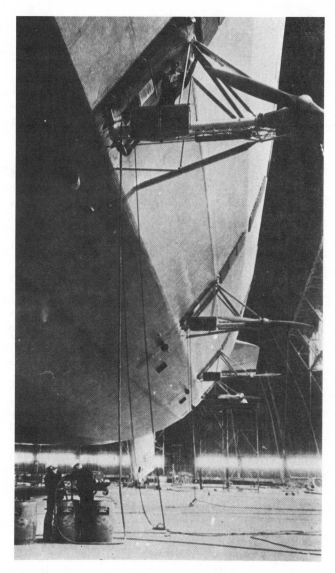

Unlike her sister ship's arrangement of radiators housed on the hull, the *Akron's* radiators are on the propeller outrigger. *National Archives photo.*

upper clouds were fairly well stratified. Someone in the car indicated two thunderheads were sighted, but Wiley couldn't see them. The upper layer of clouds in the aerial sandwich through which they were flying was at 6,000 feet.

Back at Lakehurst in the cottage by the Lake, Frances Dugan sat writing her mother sometime after 10 p.m. She wrote about the hurried dinner and that "Red" would be away for several days. "But the furnace fire won't be hard to tend, and there is the book group tomorrow.

"It's thundering and lightening now, but I must remember that the *Akron* is not in it probably; and even if she were, it would make no difference. There is some Admiral and his guests aboard tonight."

She then went on to talk about the certainty of a 15 per cent pay cut, no promotion pay and the fact that "Red" would have but two weeks vacation. She concluded with the news that the *Akron* might spend the summer on the west coast.

Jagged, brilliant lightning strikes, each generating enough electricity to supply a home like Lt. Jim Dugan's for its monthly power needs, began blinding the eyes of those in the control car. Accustomed to the darkness, the men were blinded for ten seconds at a time. It was April, a height of thunderstorm activity. The storm that had started in Washington had caught up with the ship.

"Lucky" Deal had left the elevator wheel and was on duty observing another elevator man, ready to lend assistance until 11 p.m., when he would be relieved. He was glad to see 28-year old Moody Erwin, Aviation Metalsmith 2nd Class take the wheel then, with Ralph Stine, Quartermaster 1st Class standing by.

At 11:15 p.m. McCord turned to Wiley.

"Go up and have a look at the weather map," McCord ordered. Wiley went to the aerological office above the control car and talked with Lt. Herb Wescoat, who indicated he had been conversing with McCord intermittently during the evening.

"How much of a map did you get?" Wiley asked.

"About two-thirds, sir," said Wescoat.

The two-thirds had been sent in code words about 9:40 p.m. Far from the *Akron's* fateful location, in Los Angeles, a young forecaster named Irving P. Krick had just made his map for Western Air Express. He told the operations manager that he would hate to be flying off the New Jersey coast that night. He knew that a major storm system could emerge from an insignificant beginning.

Wiley glanced at the map hastily. Westcoat pointed to the storm in Washington. Wiley noticed a pressure drop of two-tenths inches below their present pressure. He reported his findings to McCord.

"I prefer to take her over the sea," McCord said. "We'll run east and then southeast and get ahead of the storm."

The eastward course had run for an hour, and then McCord ordered a 180 degree change to the rudderman.

The navigator, LCdr. Harold MacLellan, had been assuming a southeast wind, but being unable to see the surface, this guesstimate was made on an earlier sighting. However, the *Akron* arrived back at the coast earlier than he anticipated. Now he assumed that the wind was from the northeast.

Looking down, LCdr. Wiley saw a coastal town's lights through the swirling fog, 1,600 feet below.

"Change course to 120 degrees true," ordered McCord. None of the officers knew their exact position as the ship's clock showed midnight. The watch changed. Moody Erwin went for a cup of coffee, and not long after went to his bunk. He removed his leather coat and shoes and lay down with his clothes on.

"Lucky" Deal at midnight went to the smoking room with Ralph Stine. Then, he went to his bunk, three bunks astern of Erwin's. It had been a long night. He lay face outward on his outer bunk. Above him, he noted the giant No. 7 cell was surging more than normally.

A half-hour after midnight, LCdr. Wiley and the others in the control car felt the shudder and the vibration of turbulent air. Captain McCord and Wiley had been rapidly exchanging places, trying to determine from which direction the lightning was flashing more strongly so they could guide the ship away from the violent signals. A call had gone out to get Bill Boswell at the elevators—the *Shenandoah* survivor and veteran of the *ZR-2* testing in England was sorely needed. Meanwhile, Tony Swidersky and Joe Zimkus were struggling with the wheel, which at one point spun out of their hands. Lt. Richard Cross was busy with the engine telegraph signals. Lt. Morgan Redfield, the round-faced officer of the deck stood by, ready to render assistance or carry out any order as the airship struggled in the bowels of the storm.

Chief Radioman Robert Copeland kept sending messages at his post above the control car. Newark and Washington radio stations guarding 3,105 kilocycles picked up faint continuous wave (code) at 12:06, 12:13, 12:18 and 12:35 a.m.

"The ship is falling rapidly, sir," came from either Zimkus or Swidersky at the elevators. In the confusion, Wiley did not know which one reported—he could see the altimeter, which had been indicating 1,600 feet, was now 1,100 and unwinding swiftly. The ship was going down, with the bow inclined downward.

"Should I drop more ballast, Captain?" Wiley asked.

"Yes, immediately," McCord answered.

Wiley valved ballast from the service ballast bags near amidship. The ship reached 800 feet. Wiley quickly dropped emergency ballast farther forward, at frame 187. Nearly two tons of water splashed out, to mingle with the wind, rain and ocean. The forward emergency bags stopped the descent at 700 feet and the ship rose rapidly to 1,300 feet.

"Reduce the rate of rise," Wiley ordered the elevator men.

Gradually, the ship reached 1,600 feet indicated altitude. While Wiley had been dropping ballast, McCord had ordered full speed on the engines. Lt. Richard Cross had relayed the signal. The eight Maybach engines struggled to provide dynamic lift and succeeded.

Only a minute or two of level flying was to be the lot of the half-dozen men in the control car. Suddenly, turbulent air returned. Wiley sensed the loss of altitude in his feet, as did the others. All knew they were in the storm's center now, at the peril of vigorous down currents.

Wiley sang, "Sound landing stations." A series of five squawks sang out at the 18 telephone stations. Lt. George Calnan appeared, and Wiley told him where ballast had been dropped. Captain McCord was at the port window, Wiley now conning the rudder man. Suddenly, the *Akron* took a sharp lurch. The rudder control wires of one rudder carried away. In two or three seconds, Wiley felt what he thought was a gust similar to ones he was accustomed to having take half a minute to pass. In three seconds it was gone. Unlike a gust, however, no air was flowing through the open windows.

"Eight hundred feet," Lt. Calnan called out laconically. Calnan dropped more water ballast.

Wiley saw his other rudder control carry away. The sound of sheaves breaking told Wiley that the ship's structure had broken somewhere aft.

Unbeknownst to the men of the *Akron*, the upper fin was being torn apart by the gusty, turbulent wind forces of the severe thunderstorm. The vertical fin at the top of the stern could carry less load than the lower fin, and once it began carrying away in the final minutes, girders with jagged edges pierced the aft cells. Helium surged from gaping rents, lift was quickly lost and the stern fell rapidly toward the waves below.

"Standard speed, all engines," McCord ordered. No sense adding to the strain on the ship now.

Wiley looked at Lt. Cross and saw that some of the engine telegraph control wires had snapped apart. The up angle at the bow was increasing, and the ship was falling rapidly. He thought both bow and stern were in an upward angle, and the ship had broken in two, He awaited the shock of the stern hitting the water. It never came.

"Altitude 300 feet," Lt. Calnan reported. Simultaneously, Wiley sighted the waves as the fog rolled away.

"Stand by for a crash," yelled Wiley. They were 200 feet from the water. All were silent in the control car.

Up in the ship's structure, Chief Boatswain's Mate Carl Dean had felt the bow go up alarmingly. "All hands forward," he called, wanting to get men from their bunks and their weight where it would do some good. Those who heard him climbed simian-like up the catwalk, fighting the 25 degree up angle.

Dick Deal felt the sideways lurch and saw longitudinal girders 7 and 8 give way. Ten seconds before the crash, the lights went out. Deal heard a noise aft. He followed Dean's order leaving his bunk at frame 118. He made it to frame 170 when his feet felt the cold ocean water. He went under with the ship, somehow found himself free of it and swam frantically to clear himself further. He knew the peril of the giant "Erector Set" coming down on the men trapped inside.

Twenty-eight year old Aviation Metalsmith Second-Class Moody Erwin was in his bunk, his shoes and leather jacket off. He saw the cell overhead surge, gas swerving to the lower end. It made a popping sound. A lurch of the ship was as if some giant had pushed the ship down at the stern, and the bow went up 40 degrees. He heard Carl Dean's order and started forward. When he reached frame 148, a large gas tank along the catwalk suddenly broke.

"Look out for that tank," yelled Chief Machinist's Mate Paul Jandeck, who was among the crew clambering forward. Erwin heard it hit the catwalk. He continued climbing to frame 175. Then the lights went out and the ship hit the water. Erwin dived head first between the wires and went into the water, bursting through the thin cotton fabric cover to escape the crumbling structure overhead. Girders were snapping all around him. The cold ocean was a protective retreat. He swam down as far as he could and then to the starboard side of the ship.

During her final hour of flight, eleven men were in the *Akron's* control car. Concerned with navigating the ship were Captain McCord, LCdr. MacLellan, navigator; Lt. Wescoat, aerologist; Lt. Clendening officer of the deck during the penultimate watch and Lt. (jg) Redfield the last half hour.

Also on duty were LCdr. Wiley, exec officer; Lt. Calnan, first lieutenant; Lt. Cross, engineering officer; and three enlisted men: Joe Zimkus, BM1c and Tony Swidersky, coxswain, at the elevators, and the rudder man, whose identity was never established.

Only one of the 11 in the car was destined to survive.

The altimeter told LCdr. Wiley that the ship was going down at the rate of fourteen feet per second. The *Akron* hit much harder then Wiley expected. The ship kept on going on and under the water, the ocean sweeping rapidly through the open windows of the car. The water picked Wiley up and carried him out the port window. He swam deep under water to get from under the ship. When he surfaced in the night, the brine wind-whipped into his face, the lightning flashed. The airship drifted away rapidly. When he reached 500 yards, he saw the *Akron* was entirely on the water, broken in two or three places and submerged about a third of her diameter. The bow for about 200 feet was inclined upward about 30 degrees. He figured the wind was northeast, so he put his back to the wind and swam toward what he thought was the direction of land, some twenty miles away. After ten minutes he found a board about three feet square. He clung to it as he drifted, rain peppering his face and thick gray-white hair.

CHAPTER TEN

Flickering Lights

April 3rd, with its overcast skies, was another "blue Monday" for 34-year old Captain Carl Dalldorf. He surveyed the deck of his Danzig-registered motor tanker, *Phoebus* from the bridge. The weekend ashore in New York had been filled with the Gemütlicheit of upper Manhattan's German-speaking populace. Now that the ship was ready to sail again, Dalldorf glanced at his wrist-watch. It was two o'clock in the afternoon. He ordered the crew to cast off from the East River berth at Pier 6.

Soon the pilot was taken aboard. *Phoebus* made her way through thick weather down Ambrose Channel, bound for Tampico on the Gulf Coast of Mexico. Dalldorf wouldn't be back in his home port of Hamburg for another five weeks.

For the next couple of hours the fog kept worsening, until 4:52 p.m., when the ship dropped the pilot near the fairway buoy in real "pea soup." Under slow speed, fog signals sounding, *Phoebus* passed Ambrose Lightship to port at 5:24 p.m.

"Change course to 174 degrees" Dalldorf ordered. The helmsman acknowledged, holding within several degrees as darkness arrived quickly over the choppy sea.

By 8 p.m., the east wind was at strength three. The thick fog persisted as the hours went by. About 10:30 p.m. Dalldorf saw lightning flash for the first time, but there was no thunder. At the same time he noted a sharp drop in the barometer. Turning to the third officer standing next to him, he said:

"We might be running into something."

"Yes," came the reply. "The lightning is getting closer."

By now they could hear distant thunder. An hour passed, and the thunder and lightning became stronger, interspersed with occasional thunder showers. By 11:30 the flashes were of blinding intensity, even through the thick fog.

The captain decided to stay on the bridge until they would be out of the storm. He felt uneasy about the odd combination—a storm, in thick fog—despite his fifteen years at sea since the end of the Great War. He stayed, but at midnight the watch changed, the second officer replacing the third. Seaman Lembke, the quartermaster, held the course as ordered.

At 12:07 a.m. another merchant ship was sharing the Atlantic sealanes off the Jersey coast. On the bridge of the *Algonquin*, northbound from Miami to New York, Second Officer Mulke peered through binoculars from the bridge. The ship was steering northeast by north to make Barnegat Light Ship. Through the fog and considerable rain, Mulke heard the rumbling motors of a large aircraft overhead. For about four minutes he watched two red lights and one flashing white light. She was headed to windward, to the southeast. Mulke consulted his chart—the *Algonquin* was nine miles south-southwest of the Light Ship. The wind was about 30 knots, he judged. He didn't envy the sky voyagers making their way through the fog and considerable rain. He didn't bother asking the radioman whether any messages were received—Mulke knew "Sparks" had given up wearing the headphones several hours earlier, due to the loud static and continued lightning of the storm.

Meanwhile, aboard *Phoebus*, the three men on the bridge knew they were now in the midst of the storm. They could see St. Elmo's Fire dancing intermittently from the stern flagstaff. At thirteen minutes after the midnight watch change the wind shifted, the fog lightened. The wind had moved from the east to north. In another five minutes it was from the northwest, strength 10, bringing with

Officers who served aboard the *Akron* and were transferred to the *Macon* sit for the camera in front of the latter airship in the hangar at Sunnyvale, California. From left, seated: Lt. Anthony Danis, Lt. Howard Coulter, Lt. Calvin Bolster, LCdr. Scott Peck, LCdr. Bert Rodgers, Cdr. Alger Dresel, LCdr. E.F. Cochrane; LCdr. Donald Mackey, Lt. Charles Roland, Lt. Walter Zimmerman and Lt. Fred Trapnell. Standing from left: Chief Boatswain William Buckley, Lt. George Campbell, Lt. John Reppy, Lt. (jg) Robert Larson, Lt. Howard Young, Lt. (jg) Harold Miller, Lt. Frederick Kivette and Chief Machinist Emmett Thurman.
National Air and Space Museum photo.

the change a heavy downpour. Ten more minutes and the wind and rain subsided.

Suddenly, through the overcast sky, a flickering light appeared. Dalldorf pointed it out to the others at about 40 degrees above the horizon and two points forward of the starboard beam. It was as if a bright, fixed star was shining through the clouds. In a short instant it disappeared, only to reappear. This time the three men noticed a second flickering light.

"It must be an electrical disturbance in the atmosphere." Dalldorf commented.

"Could be 'spooks'," the second officer remarked.

A third light now appeared, all three a light blue. Unlike the first two lights, this one flickered softly and was brighter than the other two, which were of the same intensity. The three lights equidistant from each other moved slowly toward the horizon, the brighter light flickering irregularly. The lights sometimes disappeared entirely then just as suddenly reappeared.

"I can't figure it out," said Dalldorf.

"Nor I," said the second officer.

Despite the strong intermittent lightning the men could see nothing skyward because of the heavy rain.

Now, about ten degrees over the horizon, the same lights disappeared again. But visibility improved and two points forward of the starboard beam, more bright lights blinked on the water.

"Half speed on the engines," Dalldorf ordered.

The lights in the air had become bright and yellowish.

"Probably an aircraft has fallen," Dalldorf remarked. "Fix our position."

The second officer determined they were at Latitude 39 degrees, 40 minutes North; Longitude 73 degrees 40 minutes West.

"Rudder hard starboard, engines full ahead" Dalldorf told the other officer. He signalled the engineering force below decks. It was now 12:35 a.m. Tuesday and Phoebus rushed directly toward the accident.

"Wake the crew, prepare to lower Lifeboat Number One," the Captain ordered calmly. "Have life preservers, belts and lines brough on deck. Signal 'Man Overboard' and lower boats."

The second officer gave the siren signals as ordered.

Several minutes passed after changing course. To starboard, Dalldorf could see large pools of oil and fuel in the ocean.

"Smell those fumes" the second officer said. "It's gasoline!"

Suddenly there came cries from the twelve-foot high waves in the darkness.

"Stop all engines" the captain ordered. "Turn on all deck lights."

In the lightstream to starboard the men of the Phoebus saw wreckage floating: gas tanks, with aluminium girders, mattresses, pillows, paper plates, pieces of wood, and a damaged 14-man capacity rubber raft, which was empty.

Dalldorf's watch showed 12:48 a.m. In another seven minutes the first lifeboat, carrying First Officer Richard Ceglarski and seven seamen, was lowered into the heaving sea.

Ceglarski's men in the lifeboat were directed to a large gas tank, from which they hauled aboard three water-soaked survivors. One of them, the name R. Deal stencilled on his shirt, had a broken finger from holding the tank's broken fuel line spout so it wouldn't fill with water. Deal told Ceglarski that the other men were Radioman Copeland and Moody Erwin, an Aviation Metal-smith 1st, all from the airship U.S.S. Akron. Erwin passed out as they pulled him into the boat; Copeland was already unconscious—they had to pry his fingers loose from the tank.

From the Phoebus a line was thrown to a burly, gray-haired survivor who was holding onto the damaged rubber raft. He clutched the line under his arms, and once aboard, identified himself as Lieutenant Commander Herbert V. Wiley, executive officer of the stricken airship.

Astern of Phoebus came more cries for help from men in the water. Before either the ship or the lifeboat could get to them, they had disappeared beneath the surface. By 1:10 a.m., Dalldorf launched a second lifeboat, which searched the area up to two sea miles from the ship.

It soon appeared clear that any others in the water had by now succumbed from inhaling fumes, swallowing gasoline, or having been in the forty-degree water for more than an hour-and-a-half.

The water was partially covered with fuel. An open flame would have set it ablaze.

Several water-activated automatic flares went off in the control car lighting the heaving sea as they shot 50 feet into the air. Then all was dark again.

The men of the Phoebus rubbed each of the four

men saved, put hot water bottles on them and encouraged them to drink as much cognac, whisky or port wine as they could. Deal finished off an entire fifth of whiskey and finally felt much better. Erwin, when he came to, had hallucinations and smashed a bottle from the German who offered it to him, at the same time tearing up the officer's hat. Then he passed out again.

Lt. Cdr. Wiley, his khaki uniform hung up to dry, wore a borrowed bathrobe as he prepared a wireless message in the radio room to be sent to the Navy Department. Coming out of shock, Wiley told Dalldorf there had been 76 officers and men on the *Akron*.

"Something aft must have broken," Wiley mumbled, his words dropping off at the end of the sentence. "Our steering cables parted—she didn't respond to controls."

Seaman Deal, nicknamed "Lucky" because he had missed the ill-fated flight of the *U.S.S. Shenandoah* eight years earlier, got along splendidly with the Germans. He told them he was lighting his pipe and noticed the airship was falling into the ocean at a rate of about eight hundred feet a minute. He had gulped a quick breath and then found himself in the ocean.

At 5:45 a.m. the Coast Guard ship *Tucker* arrived, and her doctor pronounced Radioman Copeland dead. Soon two more relief ships, the cruiser *Portland* (which happened to be anchored at Gravesend Bay) and an amphibian plane arrived. The three survivors and the dead man were put aboard the *Tucker* to be taken to Brooklyn Naval Hospital.

Dalldorf hoisted lifeboats at 9:12 a.m. Tuesday and continued his voyage. Arriving in Tampico eight days later, he made a report to the American Consul. To it, he appended his answer to a question cabled to the consul from the State Department in Washington on behalf of the Navy: had he heard any distress radio call from the *Akron* at any time? Dalldorf said that the radio officer of the motor tanker had gone off duty at 11 p.m., since there was so much static that there was no use working the ship's radio apparatus.

However during the hours of search and rescue, the *Phoebus* sent out 19 messages and received three times that number, most of them from press associations and individual newpapers. Dalldorf cabled his account to the Associated Press, and asked that the honorarium be given to the families of the lost men.

When the motor tanker reached Hamburg May 8, 1933, a reception was held for the officers and crew. Captain Dalldorf and First Officer Ceglarski received special honors for rescuing the three survivors of the *Akron* crash. At the reception, the German American Petroleum Company announced that Dalldorf would be given command of its soon-to-be-launched new larger tanker.

CHAPTER ELEVEN

Tragedy at Barnegat Bay

Lieutenant Commander Jesse Lloyd Kenworthy, Jr., Acting Commanding Officer of Lakehurst Naval Air Station since Commander Fred Berry had gone on the *Akron* flight, was beseiged with telephone calls and telegrams throughout Tuesday, April 4th. A former boxing contender now in his late thirties, he was used to exhibiting more than the usual in physical courage. The loss of the world's largest airship, whose sister ship, *Macon*, was not yet through trial flights, brought on a mental strain particularly to him as the man now in charge.

Among the flood of calls he received were two which said that a portion of the *Akron* was still afloat. The British ship *Panther* advised that there were 40 men clinging to the wreck, but that the ship was unable to assist.

Kenworthy had special cause to worry about the crash at sea. He had to get help to those reported 40 men quickly, hoping that still more men were also clinging to wreckage and would survive. Of the 76 men aboard, only four were accounted for so far. The only type craft that could help would be the station's *J-3* blimp.

At 1:50 a.m. the first radio communication from the German tanker *Phoebus* was received by the New York Division of the U. S. Coast Guard. The *McDougal*, from Sandy Hook; the *Hunt* from New London; the *Vigilant* and the *Reliance* from Delaware Breakwater were racing to the location given by the *Phoebus* by 2:15 a.m. The *Mojave*, 80 miles away, was hitting full speed to the scene.

But daylight April 4th had such a low cloud ceiling that no relief could be sent. Soon the ceiling raised, but the wind increased and the blimp could not be taken out of the hangar. Airplanes were able to go out at breakfast time, but were back at 9:30

a.m. They reported that visibility at sea was worse than over land—they hadn't been able to see anything. As the morning wore on and the frustrated airmen champed at the bit to get to the scene, the winds decreased and the cloud layer lifted to about 500 feet. Reports of wreckage afloat kept coming in from ships underway at sea off Barnegat inlet.

At the hangar, Lt. John Murray Thornton, head of operations of the non-rigids, had his crew get the *J-3* in readiness for undocking. Kenworthy had ordered him to stand by—the ship would go out shortly. Thornton had his men pile 40 life preservers, seven life rafts which could be quickly inflated and a coil of line into the *J-3's* open gondola.

As the morning waned, Lt. Cdr. David Cummins, tired from a two-hour flight in a plane that had returned without seeing anything, came into Kenworthy's office in the Administration Building off Lansdowne Road, opposite Hangar One. Kenworthy told Cummins he was about to order the *J-3* out on the search. Cummins said he already had started the crew on getting her out of the blimp hangar.

The *J-3*, a training blimp, with a single rudder, was the only one available, and took off at 10:45 a.m., in a wind of about ten knots from north-northwest. Cummins was on the rudder wheel and Lieutenant (junior grade) William A. Cockell was on the elevator controls. The cloud ceiling as they headed for Barnegat Light was still only between 400 and 500 feet. Next the blimp headed out some fifteen miles to sea, then patrolled following the coast south. The cloud ceiling raised slowly, the wind increasing. By noon they were nearly 18 miles due east of Atlantic City, searching for wreckage. The clouds were so low and the weather

123

so thick the shore couldn't be seen any longer. They headed westward to get back within sight of shore.

"Look at the port engine," Thornton told Cummins, over the rumble of both engines. Cummins and Cockell and the four other men aboard needed no advice that the engine was running rough. As they headed back to the coast and the wind increased, the port engine started vibrating.

"Let's shut her down and reinforce the strut," Cummins said. All could see that one of the molybdenum steel struts securing the engine to the port outrigger had broken through a welded joint.

Aviation Chief Metalsmith Pasquale Bettio, at 42 the oldest man aboard, took part of the coil of line and lashed the motor to the outrigger. The wind was now up to forty knots. Since the ship had a maximum speed of 53 knots they needed the port engine going again to make headway; so they started the lashed engine and put it at two-thirds speed. The vibration was greatly reduced, but the men knew it was a matter of conjecture as to how long before its fuel line would break from the remaining vibration.

A number of Coast Guard flying boats had entered the search at daybreak. The flying boat *Sirius* with LCdr. Elmer F. Stone piloting, took off from Anacostia at 10:45 a.m. Reaching Cape May, and then Barnegat, the plane soon was passing the *J-3* blimp, whose crew waved a greeting.

"If the least thing goes wrong with that blimp," Stone remarked to his co-pilot "there'll be another airship down."

While the blimp labored against the wind, travelling crabwise, Charles Carlton, a local stone mason, was at the foot of Center Street in Beach Haven with two friends. They watched as the wind forced the gray bag, with the men in the underslung gondola trying desperately to reach shore, so it had to travel parallel to the bar. A red flag fluttered from the control car, and for several tense moments the blimp seemed to be standing still. Carlton ran toward the stricken blimp to join the crowd and grab the line the men in the blimp pointed to.

With the starboard engine at full speed and the port one at two-thirds, they were making only five miles an hour groundspeed. By the time they reached Beach Haven, a strip of land fifteen miles from the mainland at the southern end of Barnegat Bay, the *J-3* was practically at a standstill, making zero groundspeed. Thorton, Cummins and the

remaining men all knew they could never reach the mainland in the increased wind force. More than fifty Beach Haven residents were clustered below, watching the distressed blimp. Thornton ordered dropping a trail rope.

"Hold on and act as an anchor," Cummins yelled to the crowd, pointing to the rope. The crew started ripping the rip cord to let gas out of the bag through a panel at the *J-3's* top, as Thornton had decided to try for a controlled landing.

Suddenly, as they were ripping, a gust carried the blimp broadside to starboard, as they limped along fifty feet above ground, with some 25 people hanging on to the drag rope. But the rope was carried toward a power line, and the people let go beforehand. A gust at that time threw the ship to the ground, and before it hit, Thornton cut both engines. With a resounding crunch the *J-3* struck, and the big bag started deflating. As she did so, she bounced a hundred feet into the air. With engines off, the 45 knot wind carried the *J-3* swiftly out to sea, the people having let go the line in panic. Helium expelling, the blimp struck the water violently a hundred yards out from land. Cummins, the only man on board wearing a life preserver, was thrown out into the choppy sea. The big bag with its remaining six men clinging desparately to the swinging gondola bounced from the water up forty feet in the air, struck again and bounced 20 feet. On the third plunge into the sea, a half mile from shore, the remaining crew members were thrown out.

The *J-3* stayed in the water, a half-mile from shore. Chief Pasquale Bettio received intracranial injuries when his head struck part of the gondola from the sharp impact with the ocean. Cummins, who had been thrown out on the first bounce, was far from the rest of the crew. Two officers, Thornton and Cockell, together with Aviation Machinist's Mate Walter Myers, quickly inflated a raft and were hanging to it in the choppy seas. Chief Radioman Harley Manly clung to the coil of line they had brought to rescue *Akron* survivors if they located them. It was floating in the waves. Aviation Machinist's Mate First Class Kensel Sprague was swimming for the raft and soon joined the three men clinging to it.

While the forward part of the blimp was completely deflated, helium remained in the stern and she floated, tossing up and down with the rough sea.

A twin-engine Savoia-Marchetti police

amphibian was being refueled on the bay side of Long Beach pier not far away. The two flying sergeant pilots were aware of the *J-3's* difficulties, so they hastily completed refueling, took off, circled and landed close by and hauled five men aboard, carrying several between the pontoons: While Sergeant Forsythe started the engines again, Sgt. Kafka was seeing that the men were secure to the outside of the plane. In his zeal to watch the men, his hand got too close to the spinning prop. He wrapped a garment around a bleeding badly cut hand as they taxied off looking for Bettio and Cummins.

When they reached Bettio, it was apparent that he wouldn't survive the severe blow to his head. By this time, LCdr. Stone landed the Coast Guard flying boat *Sirius* in the rough seas. After a half-hour struggle with the heavy sea, his crew took aboard the limp form of LCdr. Cummins, alive but unconscious. LCdr. Stone flew the Arkansas-born Cummins to the hospital at Atlantic City, but the *J-3's* captain died enroute from having taken in too much salt water.

Back at Lakehurst, when news was received of the two deaths, Dorothy Cummins ran in to the assembled grieving wives who were awaiting more word about the *Akron*.

"Well, I'm one of you now," she said, tears streaming down her face. "My husband has drowned in the crash of the *J-3* off Beach Haven!"

The melancholy group, representing 133 fatherless children, welcomed Dot Cummins with open arms.

That same day, in Atlantic City, Erwin Cameron closed his Atlantic Machine Supply Company and set out to do what he cold to help locate the survivors of the *Akron*. He was retired from the Navy after having served as a machinest's mate for 18 years, but he still had a fond feeling of *esprit de corps* with his fellow men in blue. He knew there was a new Kellett Autogiro out at Bader Field, an airport not far from the boardwalk. He drove there and located Bill McCormick, the pilot who offered the revolutionary aircraft for hire.

"I've got fifty dollars to invest in flying out to find the men of the *Akron*," Cameron said. "How much time will that buy?"

McCormick said the cost of the autogiro was high because of its special capabilities.

"That's what I charge for an hour, but I'll give you a couple of hours, since it is for such a worthy cause."

Cameron insisted on paying the money cash in advance. Then, armed with a maritime map, he climbed into one cockpit, carrying his Brownie Number Two Camera, and McCormick started the overhead blades rotating to give helicopter-like lift and with a short run from the traditional prop in front they were airborne and flying up Albany Avenue Boulevard at a thousand feet after departing at 1:10 p.m.

By 1:20 they were over the Steel Pier and heading out to sea. Over the water, since visibility was less than overland, they dropped to six hundred feet. By 1:40 p.m. they reached Barnegat Light Ship. Flying eight miles out to sea, they passed a number of ships and floating pieces of wood, which he thought could be the tops of oil cases.

This was the perfect search vehicle, Cameron thought, as they passed several Navy seaplanes heading south at close to a hundred miles an hour. The autogiro could fly at 20 miles an hour if it wanted to look closely at anything floating, while the planes had to rush by at five times the speed. Cameron took snapshots of anything of interest, including the tide streaking directly off Beach Haven after high tide. When they returned to Atlantic City after two hours and ten minutes in the air, he felt his small contribution had been worthwhile, even though they didn't spot anyone swimming or clinging to wreckage as he had hoped.

Pilot McCormick warmly shook his customer's hand. Then he went to his typewriter and wrote the Navy Department, praising the spirit of the retired man for doing what he could in the search for the lost men.

Meanwhile, five miles further out than they had flown, more ships assembled to comb the area for the wreck. The crash had been marked by the *Phoebus* as 13 miles east of Barnegat City—75 miles east of Philadelphia, between New York and Atlantic City.

The cruiser *Portland* was in charge at the scene, pending arrival of Captain Robert White, commanding Destroyer Squadron Ten. As the hours went by, a *rendez-vous* was made by four Coast Guard vessels and the Naval ships *Sagamore, Cole, Owl, Bernadou* and *Kalmia*. Sixteen seaplanes, some of them amphibians, and a dozen landplanes were assigned to the search from the local area,

Chief Radioman Robert Copeland at his station aboard the *Akron*.
National Archives photo.

Annapolis, Norfolk and Anacostia Naval Air Station in Washington. The sea was still rough and the airplane search failed to turn up any signs of survivors. For the next several days, the men of the salvage flotilla combed the heaving seas in what seemed a fruitless task.

On Thursday April 6, the third day after the crash, two oil slicks were found. A measure of encouragement was found in the arrival that day of the submarine rescue vessel *Falcon*, which had by far the most experience in this type activity. On that day a half-dozen VP-10F planes from Norfolk were sent back to their base. They were still in an experimental status, had developed engine problems and it was thought best not to risk further tragedy by exposing unproven aircraft to that duty.

Several more days went by, with the search extended systematically more than a hundred miles from the point of the crash. Sunday, April 9, the Coast Guard Cutter 213 picked up the first body—at 12:45 p.m., 22 miles east of the shoreline. It was that of LCdr. Harold MacLellan, the *Akron's* navigator. Hopes were brightened that more would surface, to be brought to shore for funeral services.

Not long after, two more officers' bodies were picked up, four miles apart and 28 miles Southeast of Barnegat Lightship—8 miles from where the *Akron* fell. They were Cdr. Frank McCord, captain of the airship, and Cdr. Fred Berry, commanding officer at Lakehurst.

On Monday, a full week after the final flight, the remains of the Navy's beloved RADM. William A. Moffett were found by a Coast Guard Cutter at 9:15 a.m., 35 miles southeast of Barnegat Light, Latitude 39:23N, Longitude 73:32 West.

The search had been hampered by heavy seas, and the weather gave no signs of improving significantly.

On the ninth day of the search, the Naval vessel *Owl* picked up a flying coat containing a pair of gloves with the name *Dugan* stencilled inside. One of the pockets carried an aviator's flight log book with notations of the flights, times of takeoff, record of ballast, amount of "super heat", etc. A tab on the flight log kept the contents locked and the inside pages did not get hurt by any water, despite nine days in the Atlantic inside the flying coat. It was presumed that the coat's owner, Lt. Hammond James Dugan, U.S.N., had gone off duty

at midnight. Since his coat was removed, he had probably been in a deep sleep after the considerable walking undertaken as assistant engineering officer. He could have perished without waking in the quick crumpling of the airship.

The first significant piece recovered was on the 13th day, April 16. The trawler *Olympia* picked up in her drag a large section of fabric from the outer cover of the *Akron*. The day following, more fabric was picked up. The grapnel also brought up a wire-entangled, headless body, but a wave washed it off before it could be recovered. Seventeen feet of steel wire swathed the body, to which only fragments of blue clung as clothing. In the same spot, a short while later that day, a regulation undershirt, and a pair of white trousers marked *Mario Ordonez* surfaced.

Finally on the fifteenth day, April 18, the wreck was located 25 miles from Barnegat Inlet Light, at 140 degrees True, in 17 fathoms depth. Divers from the *Falcon*, who had worked on the recovery of the submarines *S-4* and *S-51*, were sent below. The two experts reported many fragments on the bottom.

The first diver reported the airship's duralumin carcass was lying with a northeast heading, indicating she had weathercocked and sunk with her bow facing the wind's direction. The divers brought up books and instruments from the control car, among them two bubble sextants and two pair of binoculars.

As the diving and dragging continued, it was determined that no major portion was missing. A large section of the starboard side of the control car was brought up April 19th, but revealed nothing peculiar. The car was a hundred feet from the nearest point of the main body of the airship. Four days of poor weather followed.

On Monday, April 24—three weeks after the *Akron* started her last flight—a diver located the lower fin, some 200 feet from the main body of wreckage. He had followed deep ridges in the ocean bed to the missing fin. The other diver had gone down 80 feet on a 105 foot long line lying on the bottom. There he appraised the mass of tangled sharp, jagged frames of duralumin and loose wires and reported that the wreck was torn like an egg shell.

The two highly experienced divers talked it over with the *Falcon's* skipper.

"It will be impossible to recover any bodies," said one diver. "Under that death trap there's just a lot of decomposition—muscilaginous or subcutaneous matter."

"Yes," the captain agreed. "No use risking your lives further—after three weeks in the ocean, there's not much left. I'll recommend to Captain White that further salvage be discontinued.

The other diver breathed a sigh of relief. The weather had been rough for the operation more than half the time. The miscellaneous items recovered were tagged and sent back to Lakehurst for the Court of Inquiry.

The Aviator's Flight Log belonging to Lt. Hammond James Dugan, U.S.N., eventually was given to his widow. Its leather wraparound cover and contents show no trace of water from the Atlantic. It now reposes with the Maryland Historical Society in its collection of "Dugan Letters," which follow the exciting training and schooling years of a brilliant young man with boundless enthusiasm for the promise of large rigid airships.

Within two months of the end of salvage operations, a department store in Baltimore, Dugan's home town, was displaying a service cap with a blue cover and a Captain's-Commander's visor. A card alleged that it belonged to the late Cdr. Frank C. McCord, and that it had been picked up near Wachaprague, Virginia.

When word reached the new Chief of the Bureau of Aeronautics, Rear Admiral E. J. King gave orders that the cap be picked up as Navy property and be forwarded to Lakehurst Naval Air Station without delay. Admiral King also saw to it that the many letters from the public and from Congressmen, requesting souvenirs of the airship as parts of collections or other purposes, were answered in standard fashion. No parts of the airship would be made available.

The National Air and space Museum of the Smithsonian Institute eventually was given a box-girder section from the airship to exhibit, in comparison with a triangular girder from the *U.S.S. Shenandoah.*

The wreck of the *J-3* blimp while searching for *Akron* survivors. *National Archives photo.*

CHAPTER TWELVE

Fin Design

There has always been a sizeable group which has believed that the official finding of the loss of the *Akron* is not as plausible as it appeared at the time, in view of what happened subsequently to her sister ship, the *Macon*. The official report, as amplified by several articles written by Cdr. C. E. Rosendahl, reported that the *Akron* was too close to the surface of the ocean in the severe storm of April 3, 1933. She had insufficient maneuvering room, and was literally flown into the angry seas. Possibly. But there is considerable evidence to the contrary, including as yet unpublished theories by those who at first subscribed to the official finding and now have changed their theory.

The fins were eleven feet thick, and 41 feet high. Aerodynamically, they presented their own problems. Even a layman but first class reporter such as Ernie Pyle, aviation editor of the Washington *Daily News*, described the vibrations and creaking of the fins in a very early flight aboard the *Akron*.

Captain Anton Heinen, German expert who had long knowledge of airship matters and was brought to this country to train Navy men in operating the *U.S.S. Shenandoah*, thought strong turbulence could cause a fin to fail—years before it actually happened to the *Macon* off Point Sur on February 12, 1935. Under questioning during the investigation into the loss of the *Akron* by a Congressional Committee, Heinen said:

"Fins are rather large bodies of plain construction metal. They are not thin planes. They are bodies built up by constructing girders from two longitudinal girders and they come together at the trailing edge of the fin. On the inside, a large amount of air is encased tightly by the outer cover. Inside, it can be the same as when you are driving in a closed auto and you feel pressure on your ear drums. A (strong) wind causes a vacuum and with normal pressure inside and insufficient vent holes the onrush of air over the *ZR-1* increased pressure and collapsed the fin of the *Shenandoah*."

The fin collapse on the *ZR-1* while moored to the mast January 16, 1924, was complete, but Heinen and a skeleton crew brought the ship back safely after she broke away from the mast and had a wild nine-hour flight in the gale that tore her loose. His opinion was that history could have repeated itself with the *Akron*. In his testimony, Heinen pointed out that the *Graf Zeppelin* had serious fin trouble on her first flight to this country. Dr. Hugo Eckener's son and other crewmen went out on the fin and replaced outer covering that had carried away in stormy winds.

During the construction of the *Akron* there was considerable publicity given to allegations by E. C. McDonald, onetime construction supervisor, and W. B. Underwood, mechanic, that workmanship was deficient. They charged that duralumin was defective and there were hundreds of loose rivets. The Navy later got them to sign statements that neither one of them was an engineer and hence unqualified to pass judgement. Still, in preparing a brief for fin failure, one cannot dismiss completely the fact that these charges came up.

The testimony of the two enlisted survivors, who saw girders parting and heard other sounds of structural failure three minutes before the *Akron* hit the ocean were not given much weight. LCdr. Herbert V. Wiley was confused about the flight path of the ship on the last five hour flight, correcting his reconstruction of the line of flight by erasing the map and drawing a new course.

TIME magazine reported of the inquiry that

The *U.S.S. Macon* drops water ballast near the mast at the Goodyear-Zeppelin Corporation at Akron, Ohio. Note tiny figures at observation platform atop the ship.
J. Christian Fenger photo

"Wiley read his statement in a detached, hesitant manner, as if the story were a new and strange one which he had never heard before."

Part of the testimony of LCdr. Scott E. Peck, who had a total of 4,300 flying hours and had served on the *Los Angeles* and the *Akron* in a variety of positions—navigator, engineering officer, ordnance officer, executive and mooring officer, said: "I don't like to have the ship handled on the rear fin. We handled the *Los Angeles* on the after gear. The aft engine in the center of the ship is a good point for handling the ship." Peck disproved of the design feature of the ZRS-4 and ZRS-5 which put the weight and strains of handling on the after fin.

Twice within six months in 1932 the after lower fin was seriously damaged, involving sizeable cost and time to repair and replace crumpled structure. The first accident occurred February 22, the second one August 22nd. Accounts have been given in preceding chapters.

Goodyear-Zeppelin's public relations director, Hugh Allen, said three conclusions could be drawn from the Akron disaster. (1) Either the ship was not properly built, or (2) it was not properly operated, or (3) no airships can be safely flown and operated.

Allen said that the operational records of the *Graf Zeppelin* and the *Los Angeles* indicate that airships can be flown safely. His company's stress tests showed the *Akron* was stronger than any airship previously built. He concluded that insufficient emphasis was placed on thorough and long-continued training. "Our McCords are too precious not to be buttressed by the fullest possible experience," Allen thought.

Allen, and those "aboard" during the construction of the *Akron*, such as Lt. Tex Settle, did not subscribe to the fin failure theory. They felt Goodyear Zeppelin, with Dr. Arnstein contributing the greatest know-how available at the time, built the finest airship yet built, but that no airship could survive flying into the center of a thunderstorm's violent up and down currents.

LCdr. Bert Rodgers felt the *Akron* had an airworthiness far and above the *Los Angeles*. Having left the *Akron* to serve aboard the soon-to-be-delivered *Macon*, he testified along with 56 other witnesses at the congressional investigation. He did not believe that a "down current" would lead

directly to the surface. The boundary layer near the surface in the minds of most aviators would cause a down current to stop the downward travel of the airship before it smashed into the ocean.

Weather expert Charles Mitchell testified that the wind aloft was considerable, "blowing around 50 miles an hour from the southwest, over the whole area in Jersey north along the coast." The fin design was to stand side gusts to 34 miles an hour. It has been mentioned earlier that the original design called for the fins to be longer, not unlike those of the *Graf Zeppelin*, sloping more gradually into the structure of the airship and fastened securely to a main ring at the terminus. Because with the original design the officers in the control car forward would be unable to see the after emergency control in the lower fin, the fins were shortened. The appendage to the structure was no longer to be fastened to a main ring, but to a less sturdy intermediate ring, at frame 35.

As Lt. (jg) Hammond J. Dugan, lost on the *Akron*, had said of the crash of the *R-101*, "no one will ever know the real cause, because the survivors are too few, and the enlisted men do not know enough about aviation to tell." Thus so far we have itemized testimony and opinion which could be debated by those not holding to the fin failure theory.

As our strong card, then, may we produce the opinion of George A. Carroll, one of the Navy's first aerial photographers, whose account of his service aboard the *Akron's* sister ship, *U.S.S. Macon*, appeared in the October 1975 issue of "Naval Aviation News." No stranger to problems of aircraft fin failure, Carroll in 1930 was assigned to ride backwards in an F8C4 fighter plane to take motion pictures while the pilot dove the plane in full-power dives from 15,000 feet to a fast pullout at 10,000 feet. The tests were to film whether empty cartridges from the wing-mounted guns were tearing holes in the tail fabric so the design modifications should be made. He blacked out in the pullouts, but kept cranking his 35 mm Bell & Howell camera. When his films were viewed, engineers determined that it was structural weakness in the tail itself and not the ejected cartridges that tore holes in the tail fabric.

After the *Akron* was lost, Carroll was assigned to film the *Macon* in flight from every possible angle. He was not on the final flight of the *Macon*, but

Construction of one of the *Akron's* three upper fins. Each weighs 2,700 pounds when completed.
Maximum width at fin's junction with hull is 11.48 feet.
National Archives photo.

spent countless flying hours, with his "headquarters" in the after lower fin—an excellent platform location for photography. Here is how LCdr. George A. Carroll, U.S.N. (Retired), extrapolated his experience, as given the author:

"During my several flights aboard the airship *U.S.S. Macon* 1933-1935, I spent many hours in the control car taking pictures and observing the various operations by the ship's officers and the elevator- and rudder controlmen. I also spent many hours riding in the lower vertical fin, where I became aware of the movements of the tail section and the strange sounds during flight through turbulent air.

"So, from my flight hours aboard the airship *U.S.S. Macon* and knowing what happened in the structural failure to the upper fin which resulted in the loss of the airship, it is my opinion that the loss of the airship *U.S.S. Akron* was due to structural failure in the fin area while the airship was at a very low altitude and engulfed in a very severe thunderstorm with violent turbulent air currents of high force down drafts. The structural fin failure probably ruptured two or more of the helium gas cells in the tail section, which resulted in the immediate loss of lift, which with the strong down drafts in the storm caused the tail section of the airship to crash into the ocean. The eight engines were operating at their top horsepower, thus slaming the belly of the airship into the ocean in a few minutes.

"During the short time period, the airship was probably being tossed around, up-and-down, by the storm's violent turbulent air currents, while at the same time frequent flashes of lightning were occurring. McCord, Wiley and other officers in the control car were extremely busy trying to determine on which side of the airship the lightning was flashing in their effort to maneuver the airship out of the storm clouds. Also, the ship's altimeter could have indicated an incorrect altitude to the extent that the officers assumed the ship was higher than was indicated.

"So, under the severe thunderstorm's violent turbulent air conditions, I am of the opinion that the loss of the *Akron* was due to a fin structure failure, rupturing rear end helium gas cells, loss of lift and extreme down draft air currents.

"I am also of the opinion that Cdr. McCord was in command of the airship right up to the moment that he was engulfed in the ocean."

In a biography of Admiral W. A. Moffett, published and distributed by Edward Arpee in 1953, and titled, "From Frigates to Flat-Tops," Arpee appended a footnote on page 244:

"Why did the *Akron* go down? If there is any value in lay opinion, based on the stories of survivors and the experts, here it is. It is assumed that the *Akron* and the *Macon* had a structural weakness in the area in which the fins and the rear structure join together and in the framework which shaped the outer cloth cover. The weakness may have been due to the inexperience of the engineers in constructing a ship of this advanced size. Around midnight, on the night of the disaster, there was a beginning of collapse in this area, perhaps starting in the covering of the fin—just enough disintegration so that Erwin found it more difficult to steer the ship than usual. He thought the difficulty was due to the heavy soaking of rain. As the damage progressed and the ship became "heavy," the motors were speeded up to give more power to regain the cruising altitude. Possibly, increased speed caused further disintegration and steering became impossible. Broken cables tore gas cells at the stern and helium was lost rapidly in the rear end of the ship, making that end heavier than it would otherwise have been. The *Akron* instead of the normal position of descent with nose down, made her last descent nose up at 20 degrees."

Cdr. Joseph P. Norfleet, U.S. Naval Academy Class of 1910, is one of the pioneer naval aviators who was at Pensacola before World War I. You will find his picture with other pioneers such as Henry Mustin, "Putty" Read, Earle Spencer, Edward Simpson and a handful of other early birdmen in any account of the early naval flying boats and seaplanes—a tall, broad-shouldered officer who loved to fly. "Swifty" Norfleet served in France in World War I and at the end of the war he sent the plans for the captured German Zeppelin L-49 to Washington, from which with modifications the *U.S.S. Shenandoah* was built at the Naval Aircraft Factory in Philadelphia and assembled at Lakehurst. Norfleet was navigator on that airship for ten months under LCdr. Zachary Lansdowne, and then was transferred to the Bureau of Aeronautics in Washington. In correspondence May 30, 1974, to the author, his viewpoint is interesting pertaining to airship history:

"I think the *Akron* and *Macon* were badly designed in the first place. Many airships came to

Submarine rescue vessel
U.S.S. Falcon hoists inverted,
wrecked control car of the
Akron to ship's port side.
Car's port side is facing
Falcon. Landing bumper cushion
is missing. Main wreckage rests
on the bottom in 105 feet
of water, too tangled for safe
recovery without imperiling
divers.
U.S. Naval Institute photo,
by Falcon crewman.

an untimely end and mostly due to political interference. By that, I mean the insistance of overhead authority in ordering flights when the ships were not ready or against the advice of the pilots. This happened in the cases of the *Shenandoah, Akron* and *Macon*."

In the case of the *Akron*, the author is more inclined to agree with Captain Frank McCord's widow, Mrs. Margaret McCord. The specific decision for the last flight was not to go into the operation because Admiral Moffett wanted to make the flight. McCord had throughout his command of the ship demonstrated and objective of making the *Akron* perform. He would have made the flight to calibrate radio stations whether or not flag rank was aboard. Mrs. Peg McCord recalls her husband's outlook on the flight while making preparations and the Admiral's presence was not a factor. She related to the author that following the crash of the *Macon*, the fin failing due to metal fatigue when a gust caused explosion of the empennage, she refrained from acting on her reaction to speak out to naval authorities. The design failure of the *Akron's* sister ship now vindicates her husband as scapegoat for the *Akron* disaster.

Cdr. H. V. Wiley in a review of Rosendahl's book, "What About the Airship" in the July 1938 issue of "U. S. Naval Institute Proceedings," took exception to the former *Akron* captain's view that the airship had been flown into the ocean. Wiley, survivor of that crash as well as the *Macon's*, now subscribed to the theory of structural failure of the Akron's upper fin, as had been the cause of the *Macon's* loss.

When the author travelled to Noble County in Ohio to participate in the dedication of three memorial markers erected fifty years after the wreck of the *U.S.S. Shenandoah*, I learned from a reliable source that Vice Admiral Charles Rosendahl now holds the belief that the *Akron* was lost due to fin failure, and not to having been flown into the ocean due to a lack of maneuvering room and a faulty barometer which gave an incorrect altimeter reading, since barometric pressure had fallen in the storm. It was standard practice not to reset the instrument while in flight. The information was not for publication, but anyone doing a history of the *U.S.S. Akron* would be remiss not to pass over indication that the most famous airshipman harbored such a theory and would one day hopefully set the record straight by publishing his views.

When I passed this information on to the renowned airship historian, Dr. Douglas H. Robinson, he corroborated the fact that the Admiral had expressed his opinion to more than one source in recent years. On April 26, 1975, Dr. Robinson wrote in a letter to the author as follows:

"By coincidence, Admiral Rosendahl subscribes to your belief that the *Akron* was lost because of fin failure just as was the *Macon*. The theory has enjoyed much behind-the-scenes popularity through the years without ever surfacing publicly. I do not believe it myself, and do not believe that the bolting on of the fins to the heavy deep main frames is inherently weaker than bicycle wheel frames and cruciform girders. The design fault in the two ships was the last minute modification of the fin profiles and design in response to the demand that the lower fin control position be visible from the control car, an unrealistic requirement. The original design had fins of relatively narrow depth extending as far forward as main ring 35, to which the leading edges would have been securely anchored. The late modification increased their depth (and hence the leverage of lateral loads on them) while the leading edges were anchored to intermediate ring 28.75, a much flimsier attachment. Thus the attachments at ring 17.5 were loaded higher than if the fins had gone all the way forward to 35."

The case for fin failure while the *Akron* was buffeted in the severe thunderstorm April 4, 1933 was made strongest by the explosion of the *Macon's* upper fin 21 months later, on February 12, 1935. The *Akron* had a total of 1,695.8 flight hours; the *Macon* 1,798.2 hours. The difference is only 102.4 hours, the equivalent of a good month's flying. If a technical weakness is to occur in airplanes or airships, it would surface most likely within a similar total of hours. It did, but it came when the official investigation of the *Akron's* loss had been put to rest.

Norman J. Mayer, LTA Consultant at the National Aeronautics and Space Administration's Headquarters, Washington, D.C., was supportive of our theory of fin failure as the cause of the loss of the *Akron*. He very kindly gave us the following data on airship tail loads:

"The tail surfaces of the *Akron* and *Macon* differed from previous zeppelin designs in the following respects. They were larger proportionally, and their shapes were more rectangular. These differences coupled with the fact that all airship tails are "low-aspect ratio" surfaces of thick cross section, produced conditions where very accurate tail load determinations are necessary for proper design.

"The magnitude of loads on a tail surface depends on the angle of attack (the angle at which the local air stream strikes the surfaces) and the velocity of the air flow in the tail region. The stress produced in the tail structure are dependent on the magnitude and distribution of the loads on the surface.

"Although tests were made prior to the design of the *Akron* and *Macon*, these were not extensive enough to show the effects of what aerodynamicists call shed vortices, the air flow patterns generated by the hull in combination with the fins. The true magnitude and distribution of these conditions were later shown in tests run by the NACA (1932). The figure shows the shapes and location of the air pressure forces on a fin surface as measured in the wind tunnel. The suprising aspect of these data was the very high peak loads developed near the outer portions at the forward (leading) edges of the fins. Later wind tunnel tests disclosed an additional phenomenom not allowed for in design. This was what are characterized as "unsteady flow fields." Such conditions prevail at the beginning of flight through a gust, with the result that higher forces can be developed on a surface when it is first struck by a gust of sufficient magnitude than can be produced later either by the gust itself or high speed maneuvers. This later research data was not available until 1937.

"There is evidence that both the *Akron* and *Macon* suffered similar structural failures caused by gusts striking their tails and resulting in rapid deflation of the aft gas cells."

Mr. Mayer added that Mr. H. R. Liebert, Goodyear's ex-chief of preliminary design and an aerodynamicist, now deceased, confided to Mayer that from testimony and evidence from the *Akron* crash, he was convinced that the upper fin failed prior to impact.

A high-ranking Naval officer still on duty and preferring to remain anonymous used to have luncheon several times a week with the late Richard "Lucky" Deal. The time was in the 1950s,

and on occasion they discussed the different theories of the loss of the *Akron*, from which Deal had emerged in the trio surviving. As in the case of the *"Hindenburg's"* burning there was more than one theory. Deal's feeling was, "You pay your money and take your choice." His testimony at the investigation indicated clearly that he had heard sounds of destruction minutes *before* the ship hit the ocean.

Change in the barometer, indicating an altitude higher than the actual distance to the ocean below, was not a factor. Airship crews always flew with the barometer as set when they left the station, and were experienced in extrapolating the probable altitude. They never reset the aneroid barometer in flight, but made their own allowances from changes brought about by changing weather conditions. It was not a case of a "faulty barometer" or running out of maneuvering room and flying the airship into the ocean. The crew of the *Akron* was not to blame. The upper fin had disintegrated, causing the ship to descend out of control.

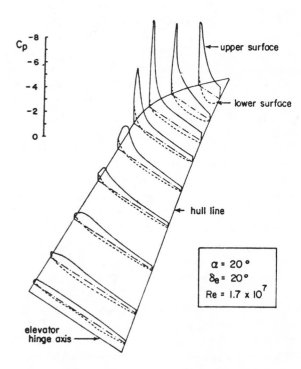

Fin Pressure Distribution Measured on $\frac{1}{40}$ Scale Model of U.S.S. Akron

CHAPTER THIRTEEN

Epilogue

Frances Smith Dugan, Margaret McCord, the other widows and the 133 fatherless children left in the wake of the *Akron's* crash had rough going following the disaster. Added to their personal grief was a depression-entangled government which the month before the crash reduced pensions for survivors of lost flying personnel by one-half.

Franny Dugan and Peg McCord organized their fellow widows in a letter-writing campaign to Congressmen to point out their plights, which fell on deaf ears. Only those who had suffered through the tragedy seemed aware of the insufficiency of living on the $21 a month that was their compensation, with a woefully inadequate $4 or $2 per child additional, depending upon the child's age. When they called on Vice President Garner's wife to elicit support, the two leaders were met with an icy reception and Mrs. Garner implied that her preparations in the kitchen had been ungraciously interrupted. Calls on their representatives proved equally unrewarding.

Thoroughly frustrated after weeks of activity in Washington, pointing out that the hazards of peacetime aviation were equally hazardous to airmen and were deserving of the compensation received prior to the act which reduced their pensions so drastically, Frances Dugan gave serious thought to picketing the White House. Hanson Baldwin, the military writer she had known since the time when he was "Red" Dugan's classmate at the Naval Academy, persuaded her that picketing would probably not be worthwhile. Mrs. William A. Moffett had even made personal calls with them on hopefully influential federal representatives. The results had been nil.

Peg McCord began picking up the pieces of her life in Washington, settling down in Chevy Chase, and pursuing her talents at gardening as an activity

as time went on. Franny Dugan completed her studies as a librarian and began working in the school system in Kentucky to raise her two children.

Seventeen days after the loss of the *Akron*, the *Macon* made her first flight. Technological improvements made the new airship a suitable standard bearer, as well as the only large rigid airship remaining to carry on for the men of Lighter-Than-Air. But technology was also improving the range and performance of flying boats and there were high-ranking officers of the Fleet who were weighing the comparative costs of the two adjuncts to operations and finding the airship costly and potentially far more expendable.

Aviation progress was never halted by a crash such as had occured to the *Akron* or earlier with the *Shenandoah*. However, as each occurred, the development of the large rigid airship for naval purposes received a severe setback.

Eight months after the loss of the *Akron*, LCdr. "Tex" Settle, U.S.N. and Major Chester L. Fordney, U. S. Marine Corps attained an altitude of 61,237 feet (11.59 miles) in the stratosphere balloon, "A Century of Progress." The flight from Akron, Ohio to Bridgeton, N.J., was to observe and record facts and phenomena in the stratosphere of interest to physicists and others. For over two hours the 600,000 cubic foot displacement balloon remained at peak altitude, while the crew attended instruments for studying cosmic and ultra-violet rays. Then gas contraction set in, and as they descended the rate ultimately reached 900 feet per minute. At 30,000 feet, disposable equipment such as radio batteries and some instruments were ballasted freely to check the rate of fall. When they finally landed safely in the marshes near Bridgeton, only 160 pounds of ballast and 15 pounds of

Dot at the top of the airship *Macon* is a Navy crewman at the observation platform. Occasion is the first flight at Akron, Ohio, April 21, 1933.
J. Christian Fenger photo.

disposable equipment remained. The flight constituted a new world's record.

The *Macon* was flown for 22 months. On February 12, 1937, a gust of wind caused her upper fin to tear off as she was flying back to base after exercises with the Fleet off Point Sur California. Cdr. Herbert V. Wiley was in command. Torn girders ripped holes in cells zero, one and two, the airship soared bow high to pressure height, and in the confusion to correct for the loss of lift in the stern, the ship flew for 34 minutes before the crash into the Pacific. Only two men lost their lives. But the Navy lost forever any further experimentation with large rigid airships. The promise of the airship the only aircraft that could cross the ocean non-stop at the time rested now with the German's new 804-foot long airship built for commercial service, the *Hindenburg*.

In Washington, less than three months before the crash of the German airship *Hindenburg* at Lakehurst May 6, 1937, Admiral Thomas C. Hart signed a 15-page Confidential Report to the Secretary of the Navy. Hart, Chairman of the Navy General Board, on February 17, 1937 directed the communication to SecNav. The subject: "Policy relative to Lighter-Then-Air ships." Composed of 32 separate items, the recommendation at the last two items called for building and maintaining non-rigid airships in numbers and classes adequate for coastal patrol and other naval purposes. The Board called for exploration of possibilities of developing rigid airships to meet naval requirements, to co-operate with other agencies in developing large commercial airships and to continue personnel training.

The program, for the immediate future, recommended (a) building two non-rigid airships per year, and (b) building one rigid airship for training and development purposes, of about 3,000,000 cubic feet and able to carry at least two airplanes.

The path through the first 14 pages leading to the recommendations in conclusion was rocky, facing head-on the negative aspects of the program as it had gone over the 14 years passed since the delivery of the *U.S.S. Shenandoah* in 1923. The airship had two years' service. The *Los Angeles* was decommissioned in June 1932 after seven and a half year's active service for reasons of economy. The *Akron* had been lost after a year and seven months in service. The General Board's policy report had been written two years after the loss of the *Macon*, after her service of 22 months.

With the loss of the *Macon* February 12, 1935, rigid airship activities in the Navy came to a standstill. The only LTA activities were confined to non-rigids or blimps and experimental work with the *Los Angeles*, then in a non-flight status.

Christmas Day of 1975, the motion picture "Hindenburg" was released by Universal Studios. The dramatization of the final days of the world's largest airship featured an all-star cast. While the Hollywood epic fell short in having stock scenes of "good guys" and "bad guys," the visual effects were superb. A 25-foot radio controlled model was made by the special effects department at Universal. The amazing model airship could perform 28 functions, ranging from dumping water ballast to operating a complex interior lighting system. A striking scene of riggers repairing a rip on one of the giant elevator fins as the airship flew over icebergs was filmed with breath-taking realism. The incident actually happened on the maiden voyage of the *Graf Zeppelin* but was added to the scenario of the later airship to keep the audience excited.

In addition to the 25-foot model, the film-makers constructed full-sized sets of the passenger compartments, several internal engineering and cargo areas as well as full-sized bow section. A full-sized control car replica was made for both interior and exterior shooting. Both the control car and the model were donated to the National Air and Space Museum for public display in Washington, D.C.

The story-line presented the possibility of sabotage. This lent Hollywood an angle replete with drama for good box-office results. A number of men connected with the LTA movement do not subscribe to that theory, and this writer would prefer to go along with the theory of those who actually were at Lakehurst, N.J. when the wrecking of the *Hindenburg* occurred May 6, 1937.

LCdr. Fred Tobin, U.S.N. (Retired) was then 45 years old and a Chief Boatswain's Mate. This writer visited him on a number of occasions while writing "Shenandoah Saga."

"Bull" Tobin was in charge of the ground crew and was directly under the nose of the airship with the forward party. Bow lines had been sent down, and Tobin's men had coupled them into the ground lines so that the nose could be pulled to the mooring mast.

His wife, Betty, was watching the mooring operation from their quarters several blocks away. She was looking out the window as the ship passed over their house. She saw a flame suddenly atop

Two-thirds of those aboard the ill-fated *Hindenburg* survived the disaster of May 6, 1937, a point often overlooked in the wake of the holocaust.
National Archives photo.

the tail fin. It raced down the top of the airship and then she saw and heard an explosion.

"Oh, my God, Fred is gone," she thought.

But Fred Tobin was not gone. He, too, had seen the little puff of fire come out of the *Hindenburg's* tail. He heard a "whoosh" and "whoosh-whoosh" as the cells touched off from tail to midships.

The lift gone from the tail, her nose quickly stood upward like a monument, smoke pouring out of the bow until it, too, burned—all in slightly over half-a-minute.

Tobin got tangled in his raincoat as he ran from the burning holocaust directly overhead. Then, clear, he fell from the entanglement of his coat. Throwing it off, he got up and told the Navy men; who were running from the inferno above:

"Stand fast! Navy men, stand fast!"

Tobin's nickname came from his foghorn-like bellow in giving orders nurtured over the several decades since he enlisted as a minor back before World War 1. The men heard, and they stood fast, their panic aborted.

Most of the newsreel cameramen had run from their cameras when the explosion occured. But one cameraman whose equipment was operating from his car battery captured the entire disaster, the film turning automatically while his legs took him away from danger.

Tobin feels that the fact that there was no wind to speak of was responsible for only 35 of the 97 aboard being killed. Another fatality was among the civilians who were paid a dollar apiece to help with the mooring lines. He panicked and ran right under the airship as it came down.

Because of the drizzle that day, the station advised the sirship to circle over the ocean until landing conditions improved. The *Hindenburg* killed time for two and a half hours. She was thoroughly wet when she came in, and there were thunderstorms all around. Tobin feels that it was static electricity that set off the hydrogen, which was being valved for the landing.

It was the second major airship disaster in which he had played a part. When the *Shenandoah* was torn apart by thunderstorms over Ava, Ohio September 3, 1925, he had been off-watch, asleep. He awoke covered with gasoline but able to tear his way through the ship's cotton fabric to safety. Because that airship used helium, there was no fire. As in the case of the *Hindenburg*, two-thirds of those aboard survived.

The promise of the big rigids went up with the holocaust of the *Hindenburg* wrecking May 6, 1937. Before we entered World War II, advocates were still pointing out the benefit of continuing rigid airships to scout vast areas of ocean, particularly in the Pacific to guard against the menacing Japanese fleet. Cdr. T.G.W. "Tex" Settle wrote a comprehensive article published in the "Naval Institute Proceedings" pointing out the precarious position of not having blimps, and when war came 130 K ships were built, four M ships and a number of training blimps. A total of 89,000 allied ships were protected by blimp anti-submarine escorts. In the Atlantic frontier, 77,500 ships were escorted, and 11,500 in the Pacific.

Blimps flew half-a-million hours on 55,900 operational flights. They were a valuable adjunct to the war effort. In 1954 the U. S. Navy introduced a designation system in which letters define function and identity of the craft. The prefix Z signifies Lighter-than-Air; "G" identifies Goodyear Aircraft Corp., sole supplier. Other letters are standard: "P" for patrol; "S" for search and "W" for warning.

Frances Smith Dugan, working as a librarian, raised her son and daughter and saw them respectively through Rensellaer and Vassar. Thirty years after being widowed, she remarried. Her large collection of memorabilia was given to the Maryland Historical Society.

As of the publication date of this book, Shell International of London is studying the feasibility of constructing an airship two-and-a-half times the size of the *Hindenburg*. Shell is interested in using the proposed ship of a 100,000,000 cubic feet capacity as a natural gas carrier. Helium would supply the lift, and the ship would be 1,800 feet long and 300 feet in diameter. The research, training and development effort is expected to require eight years. If the ship is completed, new generations will once again experience the unforgettable experience of seeing the majestic sky ships travelling the air ocean. A fuel-economy minded public will have the chance to benefit from the low-cost operation potential of giant airships to carry cargo.

The unique services which airships can perform are not being relegated to matters of history, to gather dust in archival files. As this book is published, the U. S. Coast Guard is funding a study by two Navy scientists to determine if lighter-than-air vehicles can perform some functions at less cost and/or more effectively than airplanes and surface units. Coast Guard functions to be analyzed include pollution surveillance, servicing of aids-to-navigation, enforcement of maritime laws and treaties, (especially fisheries surveillance in existing 12-mile limits and proposed 200-mile territorial waters) and search and rescue.

Moored outside the big hangar at Akron, Ohio, the first production *ZPG-2* airship built for the U. S. Navy by Goodyear Aircraft Corporation makes ready for its first flight March 20, 1953. It is 343 feet long, 96½ feet high and has a volume of 975,000 cubic feet. Envelope is of Neoprene-coated cotton, initially designed for anti-submarine operations. *Goodyear Photo from Daniel Goss.*

In mid-June of 1952 a *ZPN-1* airship lands after flight from Akron, Ohio. Ground crew is running for bow lines. Moored in the background is a K-type airship. *Official U. S. Navy photo.*

"Orange-peel" type doors of the Goodyear-Zeppelin airship dock are open and the *Macon* is ready for hauling out. Door design reduced wind currents experienced by Lakehurst hangar's square construction, where sharp corners doubled prevailing wind's velocity. *National Archives photo.*

A Navy *ZPG-2* from ZP-3, Lakehurst, N. J., hovers over the *U.S.S. Leyte* (CVA-32) May 5, 1955 prior to refueling at sea. Fuel was raised in a bag by means of a winch in the blimp.
Official U.S. Navy photo

Acknowledgements

To the Maryland Historical Society in Baltimore I owe the genesis of this book. The Society allowed me to research the "Dugan Letters," which Mrs. Hill P. Shine, the former Frances Lathrop Smith Dugan, deposited there in 1970. The collection, compiled by that talented librarian, contains the fluent writing of her husband, Lt. (jg) Hammond James Dugan, U.S.N., who vividly described his Lighter-Than-Air training at Lakehurst, his command of the metalclad blimp *ZMC-2,* and his flights as an officer of the *U.S.S. Akron.* For some years prior to learning of this collection, I had the opinion that a book covering that era ought to be written. Mrs. Shine's careful preservation of her husband's fine descriptive writing and numerous articles from the press and glossy photographs provided the necessary grist for our mill, and to Mrs. Shine and Lt. Dugan I owe deep gratitude.

A historically accurate treatment of the subject would have been impossible without the continued interest and assistance of Vice Admiral Thomas G. W. "Tex" Settle, U.S.N. (Retired). As he had done for my earlier book, "*Shenandoah* Saga," Admiral Settle painstakingly read each chapter of the manuscript and made numerous corrections and helpful comments. I was reluctant to ask him to review this second book about the Navy's airships before publication but did so in the interest of giving an accurate account. He unhesitatingly accepted the chore. With all readers fascinated by the enormous challenge that the officers and men of L.T.A. faced with enthusiasm and bravery, I share sincerest gratitude.

Mrs. Margaret McCord, widow of Cdr. Frank McCord, welcomed me into her home on several occasions and loaned a portrait of her husband. She put me in touch with her friend, Mrs. Hill Shine, and to both of those ladies I am indebted for information included in the book.

Admiral Moffett's son, George Moffett, of Annapolis, loaned a number of photographs, as well as the book by Edward Arpee, "From Frigates to Flattops," a biography of the beloved Chief of the Bureau of Aeronautics who lost his life on the *Akron.*

John B. Mitchell, Director of the Syms-Eaton Museum in Hampton, Virginia, sent us the manuscript of his booklet about the airship *Roma,* together with half-a-dozen pictures. Although the *Roma* was an Army airship, we included a brief account of it to show that the hazards of this branch of aviation were known by those who selected L.T.A. as a career.

Some useful photographs came "out of the blue." Mr. Daniel A. Goss, of Hiller, Pa., sent us pictures of the large blimps which followed the era of the

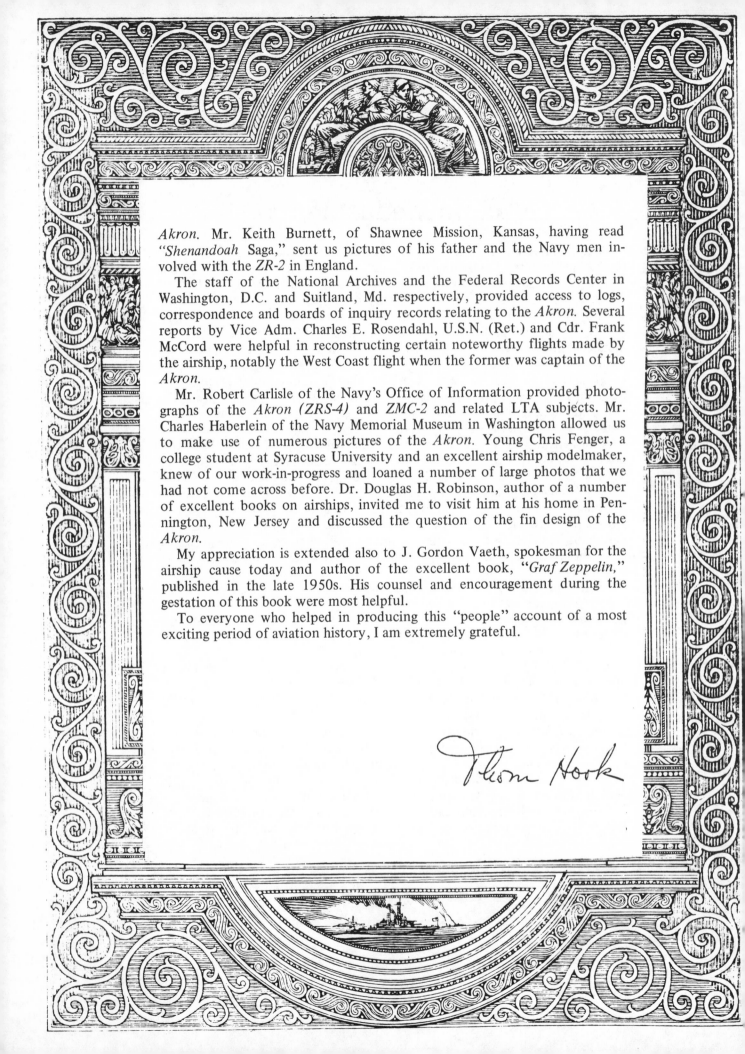

Akron. Mr. Keith Burnett, of Shawnee Mission, Kansas, having read *"Shenandoah* Saga," sent us pictures of his father and the Navy men involved with the *ZR-2* in England.

The staff of the National Archives and the Federal Records Center in Washington, D.C. and Suitland, Md. respectively, provided access to logs, correspondence and boards of inquiry records relating to the *Akron*. Several reports by Vice Adm. Charles E. Rosendahl, U.S.N. (Ret.) and Cdr. Frank McCord were helpful in reconstructing certain noteworthy flights made by the airship, notably the West Coast flight when the former was captain of the *Akron*.

Mr. Robert Carlisle of the Navy's Office of Information provided photographs of the *Akron (ZRS-4)* and *ZMC-2* and related LTA subjects. Mr. Charles Haberlein of the Navy Memorial Museum in Washington allowed us to make use of numerous pictures of the *Akron*. Young Chris Fenger, a college student at Syracuse University and an excellent airship modelmaker, knew of our work-in-progress and loaned a number of large photos that we had not come across before. Dr. Douglas H. Robinson, author of a number of excellent books on airships, invited me to visit him at his home in Pennington, New Jersey and discussed the question of the fin design of the *Akron*.

My appreciation is extended also to J. Gordon Vaeth, spokesman for the airship cause today and author of the excellent book, *"Graf Zeppelin,"* published in the late 1950s. His counsel and encouragement during the gestation of this book were most helpful.

To everyone who helped in producing this "people" account of a most exciting period of aviation history, I am extremely grateful.

Bibliography

BOOKS:

ABBOTT, Patrick "Airship–the Story of the *R-34*" Charles Scribner's Sons, New York, 1973.

ALLEN, Hugh "The Story of the Airship (Non-Rigid)," The Lakeside Press, Chicago, 1942.

AMBERS, Henry J. "The Dirigible and the Future," T. Gaus' Sons, Brooklyn, 1970.

BARNES, P. J. "Airships–Design, Construction and Uses," Office of Aeronautical Intelligence, National Advisory Committee for Aeronautics, FAA Library, 1919.

BURGESS, Charles P. "Airship Design," The Ronald Press Co., New York, 1927.

CAIDIN, Martin " Golden Wings," Random House, N.Y., 1961.

CARLISLE, CLEVELAND and WOOD "The Modern Wonder Book of the Air," The John C. Winston Co., Philadelphia, 1945.

CLARKE, Basil "The History of Airships," St. Martin's Press, New York, 1964.

COLLIER, Basil "The Airship–A History," G. P. Putnam's Sons, New York, 1974

COOKE, David C. "Dirigibles That Made History," G. P. Putnam's Sons, New York, 1962.

DENE, Shafto "Trail Blazing in the Skies," The Goodyear Tire and Rubber Co., Akron, 1943.

GLINES, Caroll V. "Lighter Than Air Flight," F. Watts, New York, 1965.

FRASER, Chelsea "Heroes of the Air," Thos. Y. Crowell, New York, 1939.

HANCOCK, Capt. Joy Bright (U.S.N., Ret.), "Lady in the Navy," The Naval Institute Press, Annapolis, 1972.

HOEHLING, A. A. "Who Destroyed the *Hindenburg?*" Little Brown & Co., New York, 1962.

HOOK, Thom "*Shenandoah* Saga," Airshow publishers, Annapolis, Md. 1973.

HORTON, Edward "The Age of the Airship", Henry Regnery Co., Chicago, 1973.

JABLONSKI, Edw. "Atlantic Fever," 866 Third Ave., New York, 1972.

JACKSON, Robt. "Airships in Peace and War," Cassell, London 1971.

KELLER, C. L., *U.S.S. Shenandoah,* (14-pages), World War I Aero Publishers, Inc., W. Roxbury, Mass.

KIRSCHNER, Edwin J. "The Zeppelin in the Atomic Age," Univ. of Illinois Press, Urbana, 1957.

MACMILLAN, Norman "Great Flights and Air Adventures," St. Martin's Press, New York, 1964.

MAITLAND, Air Commodore E. M. *R-34,* Hodder and Stoughton, London, 1920.

MOONEY, Michael M. "The *Hindenburg*," Dodd, Mead and Co. New York, 1972.

ROBINSON, Douglas *LZ-129 Hindenburg,* Morgan, Dallas, 1964.

ROSEBERRY, C. R. "The Challenging Skies," Doubleday & Co., Inc., New York, 1966.

ROSENDAHL, Charles E., "What About the Airship?" Scribner's, New York, 1938.

SETTLE, Lt. T. G. W., "Winning a Balloon Race," U. S. Naval Institute Proceedings, Annapolis, Md., August 1927.

SETTLE, LCdr. T. G. W., "The Gordon Bennett Race, 1932," U. S. Naval Institute Proceedings, Annapolis, Md., April 1933.

SMITH, Richard K. "The Airships *Akron* and *Macon*,". U. S. Naval Institute, Annapolis, 1965.

TOLAND, John "The Great Dirigibles–Their Triumphs & Disasters," Dover Publications, Inc., New York, 1972.

VAETH, J. Gordon, "When the Race for Space Began," U. S. Naval Institute Proceedings, Annapolis, Md., August 1963.

WYKES, Alan "Air Atlantic," H. Hamilton, London, 1967.

INTERVIEWS:

Mrs. Frank C. McCord, widow of Cdr. Frank McCord, U.S.N.

RAdm. Harold B. Miller, U.S.N. (ret.), HTA Unit, *U.S.S. Akron.*

VAdm. T.G.W. Settle, U.S.N. (ret.), chief naval inspector at Goodyear Zeppelin Corp., Akron, Ohio.

Cdr. Roland G. Mayer, U.S.N. (ret.), crewmember of the *Shenandoah, Akron* and *Macon.*

LCdr. Frederick J. Tobin, U.S.N. (ret.), *Shenandoah* crewman; present at *Hindenburg* disaster.

John F. McCarthy, *Shenandoah* survivor and LTA veteran.

Moody Erwin, (telephonically) *Akron* survivor.

UNPUBLISHED MATERIAL:

Letters and corresponding memoranda from the Military Records section, National Archives. Includes flight and operational reports by Cdr. Charles E. Rosendahl, now VAdm., U.S.N. (ret.) and Cdr. Frank C.McCord. Ship's Log, *U.S.S. Akron*, one volume, National Archives

PHOTOGRAPHS:

Many of the photographs are Official U.S. Navy in origin. Credit is given to our sources, as shown in captions.

INVESTIGATIONS:

"Joint Hearings with Reference to the *Akron* Disaster," 73rd Congress, U.S. Govt. Printing Office, 1933
ZRS-4 records, Federal Records, Center, Suitland, Md.

MOTION PICTURES:

"U.S.S. Akron and Hook-On Planes," exhibit films at U.S. Navy Memorial Museum, Washington, D.C.